Beginning
Evidence

Whether you're new to higher education, coming to legal study for the first time or just wondering what Evidence Law is all about, **Beginning Evidence** is the ideal introduction to help you hit the ground running. Starting with the basics and an overview of each topic, it will help you come to terms with the structure, themes and issues of the subject so that you can begin your evidence module with confidence.

Adopting a clear and simple approach with legal vocabulary explained in a detailed glossary, Dr Charanjit Singh breaks the subject of Evidence Law down using practical, everyday examples to make it understandable for anyone, whatever their background. Diagrams and flowcharts simplify complex issues, important cases are identified and explained and on-the-spot questions help you recognise potential issues or debates within the law so that you can contribute in classes with confidence.

Beginning Evidence is an ideal first introduction to the subject for LLB, GDL or ILEX students and especially international students, those enrolled on distance-learning courses or on other degree programmes.

Dr Charanjit Singh is a Barrister and Head of Undergraduate Studies in Law and Criminology at the University of West London's School of Law, is well published and has taught in Higher Education for over 13 years at both undergraduate and postgraduate levels.

Beginning the Law

A new introductory series designed to help you master the basics and progress with confidence.

Published in Spring 2014:

Beginning Employment Law, James Marson
Beginning Evidence, Dr Charanjit Singh
Beginning Human Rights, Howard Davis

Also available:

Beginning Constitutional Law, Nick Howard
Beginning Contract Law, Nicola Monaghan and Chris Monaghan
Beginning Criminal Law, Claudia Carr and Maureen Johnson
Beginning Equity and Trusts, Mohamed Ramjohn

www.routledge.com/cw/beginningthelaw

Beginning
Evidence

DR CHARANJIT SINGH

 Routledge
Taylor & Francis Group

LONDON AND NEW YORK

First published 2014
by Routledge
2 Park Square, Milton Park, Abingdon, Oxon OX14 4RN

and by Routledge
711 Third Avenue, New York, NY 10017

Routledge is an imprint of the Taylor & Francis Group, an informa business

British Library Cataloguing in Publication Data
A catalogue record for this book is available from the British Library

Library of Congress Cataloging in Publication Data
Singh, Charanjit
Beginning evidence/Charanjit Singh
  pages cm
  ISBN 978-0-415-81231-3 (hbk) – ISBN 978-0-415-81222-1 (pbk) –
  ISBN 978-1-315-79772-4 (ebk) 1. Evidence (Law)–England. I. Title.
  KD7499.6.S56 2014
  347.42'06–dc23   2013037756

ISBN: 978-0-415-81231-3 (hbk)
ISBN: 978-0-415-81222-1 (pbk)
ISBN: 978-1-315-79772-4 (ebk)

Typeset in Vectora LH and WiesbadenSwing
by Florence Production Ltd, Stoodleigh, Devon, UK

Contents

I dedicate this book to my parents and my wonderful niece and nephews: Sheetal Kaur and Sachin and Jayden Singh.

Table of Cases

Table of Legislation

Statutory Instruments

European and International Law

United States

Preface

The English law of evidence has informed the rules of many jurisdictions throughout the world and is a compulsory subject for anyone who wishes to become a practising lawyer. It is equally valuable for those that have an academic interest in the subject and for individuals that wish to improve their skills of legal analysis and reasoning. Evidence law is widely taught across LLBs throughout the United Kingdom and underpins the very essence of court advocacy; for these are the rules that govern the evidence that can be put before the court. The law of evidence is an interesting area of study because it continues to develop and it is intrinsically linked to contemporary changes in the criminal justice system, and perhaps even the measures of the changing attitudes of society as the more recent statutes, such as the Criminal Justice Act 2003, show.

This book covers the main areas of evidence law that are taught across LLBs, LLMs, BPTCs and various other courses and is essential for anyone wishing to master this subject without being baffled by legal jargon or complex and technical rules. To this endeavour the book includes diagrams, tables, on-the-spot test questions, summaries and useful further reading that will help you impress your examiners.

Beginning Evidence is written in a clear and concise manner to allow for an uncomplicated introduction to a subject that contains an intricate set of rules from the common and statutory law, and the relevant accompanying procedural rules and codes of practice. In addition to the law you will learn about the risks attached to the admission of various types of evidence and how those are mitigated, and the impact that excluding evidence has on the evidential strength of a case. The famous author Mark Twain (1835–1910) once commented that 'if you tell the truth, you don't need to remember anything'; as you will learn, this does not always ring true for witnesses, especially eyewitnesses, because of the fallibilities in the neurological faculties of human beings – thus the book also covers how the court treats particular types of evidence with caution.

Beginning Evidence is up-to-date as at September 2013 and includes discussions on the provisions of the CJA 2003 in terms of hearsay and bad character evidence, making reference to notable new cases including *R v Huhne (Christopher) and Pryce (Vasiliki)* 11th March 2013 where the trial judge's responses to the questions posed by the jurors in that case has reinvigorated the debate on jury trial and the ability of jurors in understanding their role, the trial process and drawing appropriate conclusions on the basis of the evidence that is put before them.

I would like to thank Damian Mitchell and Fiona Briden, the team at Routledge and the anonymous academic reviewers for the contribution they have made to the creation of this book.

Dr Charanjit Singh, Barrister and Head of Undergraduate Studies in
Law and Criminology at the University of West London's School of Law

Guide to the companion website

www.routledge.com/cw/beginningthelaw

Visit the *Beginning the Law* website to discover a comprehensive range of resources designed to enhance your learning experience.

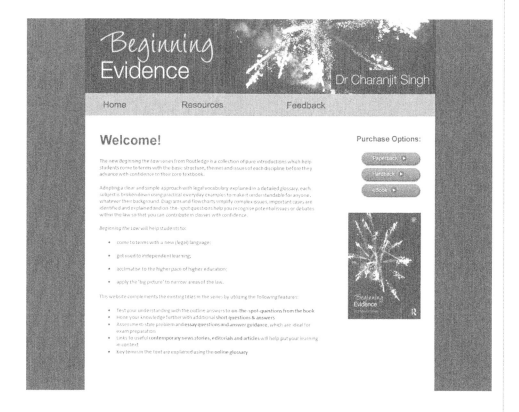

Answers to on-the-spot questions
The author's suggested answers to the questions posed in the book.

Online glossary
Reinforce your legal vocabulary with our online glossary. You can find easy to remember definitions of all key terms, listed by chapter for each title in the *Beginning the Law* series.

Chapter 1
The law of evidence: An introduction

LEARNING OUTCOMES

By the end of this chapter, you should be able to:

- Identify the basic rules of evidence law and understand how they have developed
- Critically analyse the different categories of evidence and their purpose
- Determine when and the reason why certain evidence is admissible
- Explore the rules for the exclusion of evidence
- Outline the different roles that lawyers, judges and juries play in evidence law

INTRODUCTION: WHAT IS EVIDENCE LAW?

The law of evidence is often described as a library or set of rules and exceptions that come together to help the judge and jury recreate, in their minds, what allegedly happened within a given situation. These rules govern what evidence can be put before the court (what is **admissible** and what may be *excluded*), how it should be presented at court and how facts are proven in court. **Evidence** can be defined as facts or information that indicates if a proposition is legally acceptable as being true or valid, for example the results of an alcohol blood concentration report as evidence that the accused was over the permitted legal limit while driving.

The parties to an action (whether that is the accused or the claimant/defendant) do not have automatic permission to present to the court everything that may assist their case. Parties may only present evidence to the court that is (a) relevant to a disputed fact and (b) admissible. Even if this rule is satisfied, a judge may for a number of reasons decide to exclude it.

In this chapter we will examine these rules and exceptions and consider how the law has developed as it has and why judges still retain the discretion to exclude evidence. We will also look at the different categories of evidence and then consider the roles of key legal professionals with respect to the law of evidence in England and Wales.

Figure 1.1 highlights the major types of evidence law you are likely to encounter on your own course, and which we will go on to examine in this book. The definitions that are used in the book are consistent with those you will encounter on your own course and will remain consistent throughout the book.

Figure 1.1 Evidence types

AN EXCLUSIONARY APPROACH BY THE ENGLISH COURTS

In this chapter we will look at how and why the law of evidence has developed as it has in order to understand the context of the current law.

There are many jurisdictions in which all relevant evidence is admissible. In contrast, the position in the English law of evidence is far more cautious. This cautious approach was heavily criticised because it would often result in relevant evidence being excluded. The origins of this approach lie in the concept of trial by jury and the notion that:

(a)   jurors were unable to analyse all the evidence that they were presented with;

(b)   they may assess it inappropriately by giving it more weight than it deserved; or

(c) they may be far more easily prejudiced by it if it were not excluded (public policy/ fairness).

English trial judges were also especially vigilant in excluding evidence they believed to be concocted, distorted or fabricated. There were also public policy reasons for the exclusion of evidence from disclosure, such as legal professional privilege and public interest immunity, examples of which are discussed later in the book. Hearsay evidence was also commonly excluded – as discussed in Chapter 7.

The current approach is an inclusionary one. For example, for the first time recent legislation such as the CJA 2003 statutorily provides for the inclusion of hearsay and **bad character** evidence, albeit subject to a number of safeguards. It is important to note that such evidence was admissible in certain circumstances and under particular conditions prior to this. These changes are based on a combination of logic and policy, for instance a change in the perception relating to a jury's ability to assess bad character evidence.

LAWYERS AND EVIDENCE

In England and Wales lawyers (barristers/solicitors) are instructed to act for the accused and present the evidence on an **adversarial** basis, which is in opposition to the evidence of the Crown Prosecution Service, to a judge and jury. In contrast, the continental system is **inquisitorial** where the judge acts to supervise the gathering of evidence and thus plays a far more active role in the resolution of the case.

Lawyers play a key role in preparing and presenting their client's case. When assessing the evidence the lawyer will normally ask himself or herself the following:

This is because only relevant and admissible evidence can be presented to the court. You will use the same test yourself when considering a problem question or assessment on your course.

Logically, relevance is considered first. If you are presented with ten pieces of admissible evidence, it may be that only five are relevant to the case at hand. We will see that even

Figure 1.2 Questions when assessing evidence

where five pieces of evidence are considered relevant, not all of these may be admissible; one of the reasons for this may be that the evidence was improperly obtained. For instance the Police and Criminal Evidence Act 1984 (PACE) and the PACE Codes of Practice (COP) provide a framework in relation to police powers and safeguards. The COP cover stop and search, detention and arrest, investigation and identification, and interviewing of suspects. A breach of the Codes is likely to result in evidence, although relevant and admissible, being excluded. For example the reliability of a confession will be called into question if the police fail to allow a suspect to have sufficient rest before, and during, an interview (see *R v Fulling* 1987 2 All ER 65). This will potentially breach the code of practice that relates to detention.

It is a fundamental rule of the English law of evidence that any relevant evidence that is rendered inadmissible cannot subsequently be presented to the court for consideration. This strictly applies even for evidence that might be central to a case.

CATEGORIES OF JUDICIAL EVIDENCE

Before looking at the different types of evidence, it is important to understand that a single piece of evidence can be admissible as proof of numerous things. For instance the contents of a letter will be categorised as hearsay if presented as proving the truth of its contents – perhaps it contained a threat. If the contents are inadmissible, because they do not fall into any of the categories of admissible hearsay by reason of the CJA 2003, then that same letter will not be hearsay if it is presented to contradict a defendant's claim that no communication had ever occurred between his or herself and another party to the proceedings. Therefore, students are required to have a working knowledge of how various rules apply to the same piece of evidence in a single scenario – this is discussed where relevant.

In this book, we will consider the following categories of evidence:

- Direct and circumstantial
- Original, primary and secondary
- Presumptive and conclusive
- Oral testimony
- Real and documentary

Direct and circumstantial evidence

Direct evidence does not require any further inferences to be drawn from it and usually concerns a direct perception of a fact either by sight, sound or even smell or taste. For example, if Mark saw Sian stabbing Julie with a knife, then providing the jury believed Mark, this would be direct evidence that Sian stabbed Julie.

In contrast, **circumstantial evidence** does require further inferences to be drawn. For instance, Peter's testimony that when he arrived at the scene of the crime Frank was standing over Mabel's body holding a bloodstained knife is circumstantial evidence of the fact that Frank killed Mabel because he cannot give direct evidence of this as he had not actually seen Frank stab Mabel. The inference that will be drawn is often obvious but occasionally it is not. In such a situation, other additional circumstantial evidence can be used to support the inference. For example, in the scenario above, Peter may have heard shouting and then a scream before he arrived at the scene, which may suggest that Frank had no time to flee.

When considering whether circumstantial evidence proves something or not the jury will ask itself the following questions:

(a) Does this evidence prove the relevant facts or at least some of them? If the answer to this is yes, then it will ask itself:
(b) Should the fact in issue be inferred by the existence of these relevant facts?

Other circumstantial evidence may also assist the jury in drawing an inference; Frank may have had no answer to why he was standing at the scene of the crime holding the bloodstained knife. Therefore, the jury may accept Peter's evidence that it was Frank who stabbed Mabel to death.

Key Definition

In *R v Exall* (1866) 4 F & F 922, Pollock CB describes circumstantial evidence as 'the strands of a rope that may on their own be unable to sustain the weight of whatever hangs from it but, when more than one is taken together it is of sufficient strength to step up to the task'.

We can see from the scenario above, how very apt this description is.

Primary, secondary and original evidence

The difference between primary and secondary evidence is of utmost importance where privileged documents are concerned, and we will discuss this in Chapter 5 of this book.

Key Definitions

Primary evidence is always taken to be the best sort of evidence that can be presented. Examples of primary evidence include an original mobile telephone contract agreement or the title deeds to a piece of land. Traditionally, the law always required primary evidence to be presented but the position is now far less strict.

Secondary evidence is considered inferior in comparison. Examples of secondary evidence could include a photocopy of the mobile phone contract or even a statement confirming the contents of the contract.

We will consider **hearsay** more fully in Chapter 7 but, for current purposes, it is an out-of-court statement that is presented to the court as proof of matters stated within it – for instance, evidence presented to the court by a witness who does not have first-hand knowledge of the facts they are requesting the court to believe as being true.

The categorisation and application of a particular set of rules to a piece of evidence also depend on the reason why it is being tendered. For example, Farah writes a defamatory letter to Ajay a week before she is murdered. Ajay contends that he has never had any communication with Farah. The statement can be presented for one of two purposes: (a) as an out-of-court statement that is presented to the court as proof of matters stated within it; or (b) as proof of the fact that Ajay had been in communication with Farah even though he states that they had never been. Where it is presented to the court for purpose (a) it is hearsay evidence and subject to the rules outlined in the CJA 2003 however if it is tendered for purpose (b) only then it is *original evidence* and falls outside of the hearsay rules.

Presumptive and conclusive evidence

Presumptive evidence relates to rules of law that apply unless they are successfully challenged or **rebutted**. Here basic facts give rise to a presumed fact to which the opposing party must provide evidence in contradiction if they are to successfully challenge it. Once challenged the court must determine whether or not the presumption is still applicable.

The most commonly cited example relates to the presumption of death. For example, 10 years ago Pierre left his wife Francoise to go to work and was never to be seen again (basic facts). Francoise now wishes to marry Andre but is unsure of her rights. In this instance, the presumption of death (presumed fact) will apply because Pierre has been missing for the requisite period of seven years. If however, evidence can be provided that someone has

---

KEY CASE ANALYSIS: *Woodhouse v Hall* (1980) 72 Cr App R 39

Background

The defendant had been charged with an offence contrary to s 33 of the Sexual Offences Act 1956 of having been involved in the management of a brothel. The prosecution sought to adduce the evidence of a number of police officers that had been offered sexual services (masturbation) by their masseuse during their visit to the massage parlour in exchange for money. The accused argued that this evidence was inadmissible hearsay because it was an out-of-court statement being tendered to prove that the massage parlour was a brothel and the magistrates should refuse to admit on this basis.

Principle established

The principle as set out by Lord Justice Donaldson was that the evidence was not inadmissible hearsay because it was not being presented as proof of the truth of the masseuse's statement (that a sexual act would be performed), instead it was being presented as proof that she had offered him sexual services in exchange for money.

---

heard from Pierre since then, the presumption can be rebutted. Note, when the UK's Presumption of Death Act 2013 becomes law, individuals such as Francoise will be able to apply to the High Court for a declaration that the missing person is deemed to have died.

In contrast, conclusive evidence cannot be rebutted. Thus, as the name suggests, it is conclusive. Contemporary examples of the rules of conclusive evidence include the presumption that everyone is *aware of what the law is* or that a child under the age of 10 years old is *doli incapax* (incapable of committing a crime because they are not able to form the necessary criminal intent).

Oral evidence (testimony)

Oral evidence is evidence that a witness gives in court in his or her own words as **evidence-in-chief**, **cross-examination** and **re-examination**. Evidence that is given under special measures is still considered to be oral testimony; for example the court may order that a vulnerable witness (someone under age) may give their evidence via video link. Even documents, such as affidavits or witness statements in the civil courts, are accepted as oral evidence in their own right.

Real and documentary evidence

Real evidence is tangible evidence that is observed or inspected in court, allowing the jury to draw inferences from it. A machete that had been used to murder someone would be an example of this type of evidence, or items such as photographs of a crime scene or a victim or a witness. These categories are not mutually exclusive; real evidence may be circumstantial, such as blood stains used to extract DNA evidence. The point to note is that real evidence must be something that makes an impression on the court.

Documentary evidence consists of any recorded document, including photographs and films or closed circuit television (CCTV) footage. In accordance with the best evidence rule the original document must be presented although certified copies are often acceptable as we will see later, in Chapter 10.

On-the-spot question

 Do you think that all relevant evidence should automatically be admissible?

FACTS

We will now consider the purpose of **adducing** evidence. In every set of proceedings there will be a number of facts that are in issue. The parties will therefore have to produce relevant and admissible evidence that somehow proves or disproves the fact in issue.

In a criminal case, the facts in issue will often consist of the identity of the assailant or the elements that the prosecution must establish in order to prove their case and the defendant's guilt. If a defendant raises a defence (such as self-defence, for example), that will also be in issue. It is the task of the prosecution to disprove the defence. Often the entire prosecution case will be in issue where a defendant pleads not guilty or makes a partial admission, such as an admission that they were present at the scene of the crime. When a fact in issue is admitted, it is no longer in issue and does not require any formal proof. An admission can be made by any of the parties at any time during the proceedings. The rules for formal admissions in criminal proceedings are laid out by s 10 of the Criminal Justice Act 1967 (CJA). In short, it states that formal admissions can be made at any time in writing or orally in court and that they can, with the leave of the court, be withdrawn.

In civil cases the particulars of the claim outline the facts that are in issue. These are essentially those facts upon which the claimant bases their claim.

Collateral facts are facts that affect the admissibility of the evidence that the parties are seeking to present. Collateral facts can affect the credibility of a witness or the weight that can be ascribed to a piece of evidence. For instance, if a confession is obtained through oppression then the court will decide whether this evidence can be adduced in court – the fact that it was obtained through oppressive means is a collateral fact. Often, from a procedural perspective, such evidence would be put before the court prior to it being adduced. This is usually because the opposing side has objected to its use by reason of the collateral fact.

Therefore, only relevant facts act to prove or disprove the facts that are in issue. In *DPP v Kilbourne* [1973] AC 729 Lord Simon stated that evidence is relevant where it is logically probative or **disprobative** of some matter that requires proof. Here probative is defined as the extent that the evidence affects the probability that the fact in issue or collateral fact exists. In other words, it must be evidence that proves or persuades someone that a proposition is probably true. In contrast, disprobative can be defined as the extent that the evidence affects the probability that the fact in issue or collateral fact does not exist – or evidence that proves or persuades someone that a proposition is probably untrue. The evidence in *Kilbourne* was as follows:

- evidence (group a): victims alleging sexual abuse in 1970
- evidence (group b): victims alleging sexual abuse in 1971

The trial judge directed the jury that if they 'were satisfied with the uncorroborated evidence of the second group [b], they could take it as supporting the evidence given by the first group [a]'. The Court of Appeal held that this direction was incorrect as neither of these two pieces of evidence made the existence of abuse more likely. The House of Lords disagreed; it held that there was no general rule of law that witnesses of a class requiring corroboration cannot corroborate each other. Therefore, the judge's direction was proper, conviction upheld. The effect was to take such evidence as making the other more probative; it is likely that the recurrence of abuse was a consideration. This case also substantiates the fact that relevance is fundamental to the law of evidence because it is the relevance of the piece of evidence that reveals which rules apply to its possible admission.

As we saw earlier, the basic rule of evidence is that only relevant evidence, whether direct or circumstantial, can be admitted (see *R v Turner* [1975] QB 834). The court will not admit evidence that is completely irrelevant or insufficiently relevant to a fact in issue (*R v Randall* [2004] 1 WLR 56). Furthermore, the court will refuse to hear evidence that it deems to be sufficiently relevant to a fact in issue where that fact that has already been admitted. Relevance is determined in terms of whether or not it proves (or disproves) a fact in issue. When determining relevance, a lawyer will ask himself or herself what is the fact in issue and does this evidence go towards proving or disproving it? Another way of posing the same question is as follows: what is the probative effect of this evidence? The lesser the probative effect (or relevance) of the evidence the more likely it is that the court will reject it. To do well in your evidence course, you should apply the same question in your own assessments.

KEY CASE ANALYSIS: *Hart v Lancashire and Yorkshire Railway* **(1869) 21 LT 261**

In this case the claimant was injured by a runaway train, he alleged that was caused by the negligence of the train company Yorkshire Railway. In support of his allegation the claimant sought to prove negligence through evidence that the train company had since altered the negligent practice. The court held that evidence of the changes in the train company's practices that occurred after the accident were in themselves irrelevant to the fact in issue or negligence because it served no purpose other than to prove that the company had taken steps to improve its safety standards. The court stated that '... [one cannot hold] that, [because] the world [has become wiser with age], that it was foolish before.'

KEY CASE ANALYSIS *R v Kearley* **[1992] 2 All ER 345 (HL)**

The defendant was charged with being in possession of drugs with an intention to supply. The police conducted a search of the defendant's flat in his absence. During this search they answered 15 telephone calls, 10 of which were from callers requesting drugs. In addition, nine people called at the flat to see the defendant, seven of whom also asked for drugs.

The court held that the prosecution's evidence of the telephone calls and the related conversations were admissible as relevant evidence; Kearley was subsequently convicted. He appealed to the House of Lords on the grounds that this evidence should have been excluded. The Lords ruled that some of this evidence was indeed inadmissible because it was in fact hearsay even if it was relevant.

Lord Bridge outlined that the words spoken were irrelevant because spoken words can be relevant for proving the state of mind of the maker or the listener but only when their state of mind is a fact in issue or where it is relevant to another fact that is in issue, and in this case the words of the callers and their state of mind were irrelevant as to whether or not the defendant was in fact a supplier of drugs.

Lord Ackner validly pointed out that the words were evidence that the caller (a) wished to be supplied with drugs, and (b) that the accused could supply them; it was not relevant evidence proving that the defendant either could or would supply them.

Lord Browne-Wilkinson in his dissenting judgment stated that he believed the evidence to be relevant to the fact in issue that related to the intention to supply because of the sheer number of callers that had contacted the premises for drugs, although he also admitted that this would not be conclusive as evidence to prove this point. It is important to note the decision in a similar set of circumstances is likely to be different if made under the CJA 2003.

It is important to note that the relevance of a piece of evidence is not always obvious and that its relevance may change throughout the proceedings if other evidence comes to light. Very often, the production of evidence by the prosecution is not clear. This is because the prosecution team will attempt to foresee the defences that may be put forward and therefore include evidence that would disprove them. In such cases, after a discussion with the trial judge, the court will treat this evidence as being conditionally relevant (*de bene esse*). If the defendant does not put forward the defence to which that evidence was relevant, the trial judge will direct the jury to ignore it. The prevalent issue this raises concerns prejudice. In short, the evidence may have such a prejudicial effect on the minds of the jury against the accused that it would be unrealistic to expect them to ignore it; this can result in a retrial being ordered.

On-the-spot question

 What are commonly regarded as facts in issue in a set of civil proceedings? Think of examples from particular actions for instance negligence or breach of contract.

ADMISSIBILITY, DISCRETIONARY EXCLUSION AND WEIGHT

In this part of the chapter we will look at the admissibility of evidence, the judicial discretion to exclude it and the weight that can be ascribed to it.

Admissibility is the second requirement (after relevance) that must be satisfied before evidence can be lawfully put to the court. Where relevance is connected to whether the evidence proves (or disproves) a fact in issue, admissibility relates to whether or not the evidence falls foul of the exclusionary rules in the English law of evidence, which seek to promote authenticity and fairness. As we saw earlier and we will find throughout this book, a single piece of evidence may potentially be used to try and prove a range of different things and therefore the rules that apply to its admission will also vary.

Judicial discretion in the English law of evidence is fairly straightforward because the rules are set out far more clearly. The historical view is that judges were not allowed to include evidence that was inadmissible by operation of the law. The rule against the admission of hearsay was a good example of this – although, as we saw earlier, the CJA 2003 has altered this position now. In contrast, judges are encouraged to use discretion to exclude admissible evidence in specific circumstances:

(1)   Under the common law, the court may exclude prosecution evidence where its prejudicial effect outweighs its probative worth (see *R v Sang* (1980) AC 402 and s 82(3) of the PACE Act 1984).
(2)   Under s 78 of the PACE Act 1984 the court is allowed to exclude prosecution evidence where it considers, after having had regard to all the circumstances including those in which it was obtained, that its admission would adversely affect the fairness of the proceedings.

For assessment purposes, it is important to understand the circumstances in which this discretion applies, and I will continue to highlight examples of this throughout the book.

The **weight** that is ascribed to the evidence is a matter for the court or tribunal – the magistrates in a magistrates' court or the jury in a Crown Court. The very task of ascribing weight to evidence can seem daunting but in terms of the law of evidence we must simply consider whether the evidence proves a particular conclusion. For example, is the prosecution evidence enough to prove beyond reasonable doubt that the defendant killed the victim?

The weight that the jury ascribes to a particular piece of evidence will draw on their common sense and skills of logical reasoning. The jury may decide to give a piece of evidence weight because they believe it is reliable, truthful and strong evidence or alternatively they may give it no weight and thus reject it. Therefore, the lawyer will be required to consider the likely weight to be attached to a piece of evidence. The consideration of the weight of the evidence will influence, among other things, the prosecution's decision whether to prosecute or not; whether the accused is likely to be convicted; and negotiations in civil cases. Similarly, in an assessment situation, you will need to consider the relevance and admissibility of the evidence, and also use your own discretion to consider what weight should be attributed to that evidence.

The weight of certain types of evidence has always been a cause for concern to the courts. For example, in relation to identification evidence or lies, quite specific guidance must be given to the jury (see *R v Turnbull* [1977] QB 224 and *R v Lucas* [1981] 2 All ER 1008), as we will see in Chapter 6.

On-the-spot question

 If probative evidence persuades the court that there is a higher probability that a fact in issue is probably true, why do you think that evidence whose probative worth is outweighed by its potential prejudicial effect is excluded?

THE ROLE OF THE TRIAL JUDGE AND JURY, AND QUESTIONS OF FACT AND LAW

The judge and jury both play pivotal roles in the trial process and the relevant procedure; the process highlights the distinction in their relative functions. Outlining the difference is important because this determines who decides questions of fact or law that may arise during a trial. In the magistrates' court the trial judge or the magistrates will determine any questions of fact and law that may arise but because lay magistrates are not legally qualified they will seek the counsel of their clerk (normally a lawyer) when dealing with questions of law (see Practice Direction (Justices Clerk to Court) [1981] 1 WLR 1163). In the Crown Court, the jury decides all questions of fact. It is for the judge to sum up the case to the jury.

Questions of fact often relate to the weight ascribed to the evidence or its credibility. There are two questions of fact that the trial judge will decide:

*   the definition of any unusual terms that are contained in a contractual document; and
*   any issues that relate to the law of a foreign jurisdiction.

There are also a number of other questions that arise in cases that require consideration:

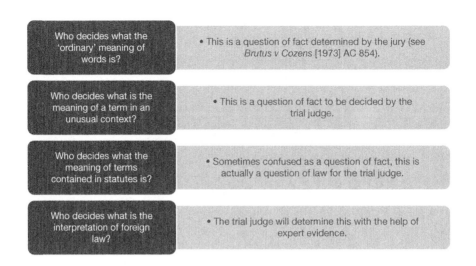

Figure 1.3 Questions of fact

You should note that even the law of Scotland is treated as foreign law for these purposes.

Questions of law relate to the definition or elements of an offence and the rules of evidence. In the event that the prosecution fails to present evidence that proves the accused has committed the offence then the lawyer for the accused will make a submission of no case to answer after the close of the prosecution case (see *R v Galbraith* [1981] 1 WLR 1039). The same judge will withdraw the case from the jury. In the magistrates' court, the position is governed by the 1962 Practice Direction issued by Lord Parker CJ in [1962] 1 WLR 227.

Questions regarding admissibility are also questions of law and are usually settled prior to the commencement of the trial. If they are not, the matter can be settled during proceedings in a *voir dire* – a procedure where the trial judge will hear the legal arguments and rule on the admissibility of a piece of evidence in absence of the jury. Where the admissibility of a piece of evidence is in issue but the trial has commenced then the lawyers would agree not to refer to it until the trial judge has ruled on its admissibility. Different rules apply where the disputed evidence is a confession, as we will see in Chapter 8. For a more detailed discussion on these rules you should refer to the Crown Court Bench Book on directions that judges give to jurors on the role of judge and jury (at pp 14–15).

On-the-spot question

 What roles do the judge and jury play in criminal proceedings?

OCCASIONS WHERE PROOF IS UNNECESSARY

There are two notable instances where proof becomes unnecessary. We have already discussed formal admissions earlier in this chapter. The other is known as judicial notice. Here the court can use its objective and general knowledge of the world and dispense with the need for evidence regarding notorious facts.

In *Lumley v Gye* (1853) 2 E & B 216 Justice Coleridge stated that judges are not ignorant of those notorious facts that those outside of court are familiar with. The reasoning is clear – there are some facts that are so well known that it would be a waste of time and money to require proof of them. For example, the fact that rain falls (*Fay v Prentice* (1845) 14 LJCP 298) and that the postal system is not always reliable (*Sloan Electronics Ltd v Customs and Excise Commissioners* [1999] unreported). Facts can be judicially noted if they are so notorious that to require proof of them would offend the common sense of judges and the honour or dignity of the court. Judges will take judicial notice of a fact automatically or after enquiry where the judge refreshes their memory (see *McQuaker v Goddard* [1940] 1 KB 687). The problems lie in the variance of common knowledge. However, the test requires judges to exercise an objective assessment in ascertaining the popularity of the facts concerned. In terms of political or international matters the court may take judicial notice so that it can act in unison with the government (see *Duff Development Company v Government of Kelantan* [1924] AC 797).

It is unclear to what extent judges and juries use their general knowledge to inform their decision making. However, where specialist knowledge (legal or otherwise) is concerned the rules are quite clear: a judge must not substitute their specialist knowledge over the requirement for evidence to prove the fact in issue. Where a judge, lay magistrate or jury member has any relevant specialised knowledge, they can be sworn in and give evidence in the standard way (see *R v Fricker* (1999) *The Times*, 13th July). In contrast, lay magistrates can rely on their professional knowledge to assess the weight of the evidence presented to them. The hallmark for judicial notice is the requirement for notoriety. Finally, statutes often provide facts of which judicial notice can be taken, for instance the Interpretation Act 1978 states that the court can take judicial notice of the fact that a copy of an Act from HM Stationery Office is accurate and reliable.

On-the-spot questions

Who decides questions of fact and law?

Do you think that there should be limitations on when a judge can rely on their specialist knowledge?

CRIMINAL AND CIVIL PROCEDURE RULES

The effect of the Civil Procedure Rules 1998 and Criminal Procedure Rules 2011 limit the evidence that is admitted for trial. The Criminal Procedure Rules (CrPR) determine how a case is managed while it progresses through the criminal justice system. In contrast, the aim of the Civil Procedure Rules is to enable cases to be dealt with justly. The rules place the responsibility of effectively managing the case on the judge, they can be downloaded at: www.justice.gov.uk/civil/procrules_fin/menus/rules.htm and www.justice.gov.uk/criminal/procrules_fin/rulesmenu.htm.

Both sets of rules seek efficiency and expeditiousness thereby encouraging communication (see *K and Others* [2006] EWCA Crim 835).

SUMMARY

Evidence law focuses on how facts are proven, how evidence is *put* before and *excluded* by the court. The purpose of this is to aid the court's understanding of what happened. When considering evidence you should begin by determining relevance first and then approach admissibility. The classification of evidence as a particular type, for example hearsay or original evidence, depends on why it has been tendered.

FURTHER READING

Cornish, WR and Sealy, AP, 'Juries and the Rules of Evidence' [1973] Crim LR 208.
This is an interesting article based on research at the London School of Economics and Political Sciences and discusses how far, if at all, it is possible to predict a juror's verdict on the basis of their age, gender or social class.

Crown Court Bench Book – Directing the Jury, Judicial Studies Board, March 2010, at pages 14–15.
Download this from: www.judiciary.gov.uk/publications-and-reports/judicial-college-Pre+2011/crown-court-bench-book-directing-the-jury. The book is written by Mr Justice Pitchford, currently a senior British Judge and Justice of the Court of Appeal of England and Wales, and brings together valuable materials used by judges to craft bespoke directions that are used in court.

Landa, CS (2012). *Evidence: Question and Answers 2013–2014*, 10th edn. London: Routledge. This essential revision guide focuses on the application of the law of evidence with some interesting practical questions and guidance on answering assessment questions.

Landa, CS and Ramjohn, M (2013). *Unlocking Evidence*. 2nd edn. London: Routledge. This textbook provides a solid introduction to the law of evidence.

Munday, R (2011). *The Law of Evidence*, 6th edn. Oxford: Oxford University Press.
Alongside *Cross & Tapper on Evidence* (2004) this is a comprehensive textbook on the law of evidence that discusses more than just the basic rules.

Ormerod, D and Birch, D, 'The Evolution of the Discretionary Exclusion of Evidence' [2004] Crim LR 767.
This is an interesting article that discusses the judicial discretion to exclude evidence and its effect.

Roberts, P and Zuckerman, A (2010). *Criminal Evidence*, 2nd edn. Oxford: Oxford University Press.
This is another good textbook on the law of criminal evidence.

Chapter 2
The burden and standard of proof

LEARNING OUTCOMES

By the end of this chapter, you should be able to:

- Understand the function of the various types of burdens of proof
- Identify and distinguish between the types of burdens of proof that exist in both civil and criminal cases
- Determine the incidence of a legal burden of proof and consider any exceptions to the general rule in criminal cases
- Critically engage with the legal principles relating to the standards of proof required in criminal and civil cases

INTRODUCTION

In Chapter 1 we discussed the various types of evidence that exist as well as their relevance and admissibility. In this chapter the discussion will focus on which party has the obligation to prove or disprove a fact that is in issue and the standard to which they must prove or disprove it.

TYPES OF BURDENS OF PROOF

The notion of 'proof' in law relates to evidence that sufficiently establishes a belief that an asserted fact is correct. For instance in most common law systems the prosecution must prove through relevant and admissible evidence that the accused is guilty.

Key Definition

Viscount Sankey established the 'golden thread' in English criminal law in *Woolmington v DPP* [1935] AC 462, he stated: 'While the prosecution must prove the guilt of the [accused] . . . there is no burden laid on the [accused] to prove his innocence and it is sufficient for him to raise doubt as to his guilt' (p 481).

The **burden of proof** relates to the established proposition that the person who asserts something must prove it. This is known as the **incidence** or occurrence of the legal burden of proof. In criminal cases an automatic presumption of innocence applies. In this instance the Latin maxim *ei incumbit probatio qui dicit, non qui negat* applies (the burden of proof lies with 'he who asserts' and not with 'he who denies'), therefore the principle is: an accused is innocent until they are proven to be guilty. The English law of evidence recognises the following two principal burdens of proof:

Legal burden	Evidential burden
The obligation on a party to prove a fact in issue. The tribunal of fact will determine whether this has been discharged at the end of the trial. Also referred to as the persuasive burden.	The obligation on a party to adduce sufficient evidence to raise a fact in issue; make it a live issue in the trial. The trial judge will assess whether the evidence is sufficient to do this. If it is not sufficient then the party cannot put the fact in issue before the trier of fact. Whether a party has discharged this burden is a question of law for the trial judge. The party who bears the legal burden also bears the evidential burden on that fact, but as you will see later there are exceptions.

Figure 2.1 Principal burdens of proof

Figure 2.2 summarises where the legal and evidential burdens of proof lie in a criminal trial:

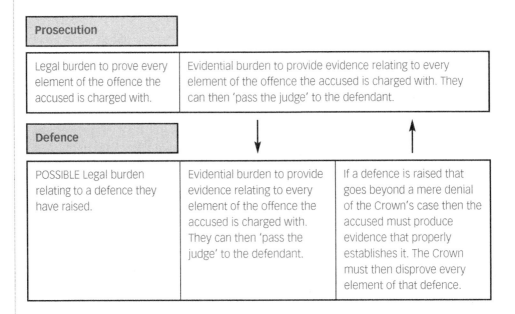

Figure 2.2 The legal and evidential burdens of proof criminal trials

In contrast, the standard of proof refers to degree of cogency or persuasiveness that is required of the evidence to discharge the legal, not the evidential, burden of proof. Therefore, the party bearing the **legal burden of proof** on a fact in issue will lose on that issue if the trier of fact decides that the evidence is not sufficient to satisfy the requisite standard of proof.

You should also note the following points: the legal burden does not shift from the prosecution to the defence and the defence does not have to disprove the Crown's case – it only has to 'raise doubt' in the mind of the trier of fact.

The persuasive burden (legal burden) of proof

The persuasive burden, also known as the legal burden, the ultimate burden and even the 'risk of non-persuasion', refers to the obligation or requirement that is placed on a party to the proceedings to prove a fact in issue. The question of whether that party has discharged the legal burden is for the tribunal of fact to decide at the end of the trial. Lord Denning coined the term 'legal burden' perhaps because the substantive law on evidence determines the decision on which party is required to satisfy it. If the tribunal of fact decides that the party bearing the legal burden of proof has failed to discharge it to its satisfaction then that party will inevitably lose their case. In criminal proceedings the Crown must satisfy the tribunal of fact beyond all reasonable doubt that the accused is guilty of committing the offence with which they are charged. If it fails to do this then the accused will of course be acquitted. Similarly, in civil proceedings, the claimant must prove on the balance of probabilities all the requisite elements of the claim i.e. duty, breach and damage, if they fail to do so then judgment will be given in the defendant's favour.

The question of which party bears the legal burden of proof is determined at the beginning of the trial and this does not change as the proceedings progress. In short, the legal burden never shifts from one party to the other. The basic rule is: the burden placed on the prosecution will remain the same throughout the trial, however a possible legal burden may be imposed on the accused for example in relation to a defence they raise. The party that bears the legal burden of proof also bears the **evidential burden of proof** – there are a number of exceptions to this.

On-the-spot question

 Summarise your understanding of the legal burden of proof.

The evidential burden of proof

The parties to the proceedings may also bear an evidential burden. This is the obligation or requirement on a party in the proceedings to adduce evidence sufficient enough to raise a fact in issue to make it a *live* issue in the trial. Whether or not that party has discharged the evidential burden is a question of law for the judge (tribunal of law) to decide. If the judge decides that the party has not discharged the evidential burden then they will not allow the issue to be put before the tribunal of fact, in the Crown Court this is the jury but in criminal cases without juries and in civil cases this will be the judge because they will be the trier of fact and law. The evidential burden has other names including a 'burden of raising' (see Lord Bingham in AG's *Reference (No 4 of 2002)* [2004] 3 WLR 976). However the former term is generally preferred (*DPP v Sheldrake* [2004] QB 487) and used in this book.

There is of course a debate as to the existence of the evidential burden of proof with many regarding it as non-existent or simply an extension or precursor to the legal burden of proof. The reasoning for this is that the party bearing the evidential burden does not have to prove anything to the tribunal of fact; it must merely adduce evidence to satisfy the trier of law. In *Jayasena v R* [1970] AC 618 Lord Devlin argued that to call this a burden of proof is misleading because it can be discharged by the production of evidence which itself can fall short of proving anything. For instance the defendant may seek to rely on discredited prosecution evidence. The following question arises: does the party bearing the evidential burden have a duty to raise an issue as part of its case or does that issue exist by reason of the facts of the case regardless of who bears the evidential burden? For instance A is charged with murder but contends that he or she was acting in self-defence, is the defence already a *live* issue in the trial? There are contrasting judicial views on this matter. Judge Edmund Davies suggests in *R v Gill* (1963) 47 Cr App R 166 that the party bearing the evidential burden has the obligation of raising the issue to make it a live one otherwise it would not form part of the proceedings. He states:

> [An] accused . . . must place before the court such material as makes [their defence] a live issue [that is] fit and proper to be left to the jury. [Once they have discharged the evidential burden] it is then for the Crown to destroy that defence . . . [so] as to leave [no reasonable doubt] in the jury's minds that the accused cannot be absolved on [those] grounds.

In contrast, Lord Tucker in *Bullard v R* [1957] AC 635 suggested that the issue is not to be left to the party bearing the evidential burden to raise it making it a live issue in the trial where he stated:

> [It is] settled law that if on the evidence, whether [that of] the prosecution or [the] defence, there is any evidence of provocation . . . whether or not this issue has been . . . raised [by the prosecution or the defence] . . . it is the duty of the judge, after proper direction, to leave it open to the jury to return a verdict of

manslaughter, if they are not satisfied beyond reasonable doubt that the killing was unprovoked.

Although this authority concerns provocation it has a broader application. In reality, where the evidence already tendered suggests the existence of a defence then it is likely that the evidential burden will have been satisfied; that is true even though that evidence may have been tendered for an alternative purpose. Thus, it is quite right that both prosecution and defence, so as to avoid a potentially unsafe and appealable conviction, directly address the matter.

On-the-spot question

 How is the evidential burden of proof defined?

Coincidence of the legal and evidential burden

The party bearing the legal burden of proof will also bear the evidential burden on that matter. There are a number of exceptions to this, including formal admissions, judicial notice and presumptions. The trier of fact will determine whether the legal burden has been discharged at the end of the trial and the trier of law decides the same in relation to the discharge of the evidential burden but before the commencement of the proceedings. It does not follow that if the evidential burden is discharged that discharge of the legal burden will also follow. In summary, discharge of the evidential burden merely supports the argument that the trier of fact may find against the opposing party on that particular issue.

One of the parties to the proceedings may bear the evidential burden on an issue but not the legal burden; an example is the defendant raising a defence. Here the defendant would adduce sufficient evidence to convince the trier of law that they should allow the jury to consider the defence.

Distinguishing between the legal and evidential burdens

It is important to distinguish between the legal and evidential burdens for assessment purposes. For instance it is the party that bears the legal burden that has the right to open the proceedings with their case. The half-time submission of 'no case to answer' concerns the discharge of the evidential burden by the party bearing the legal burden. The decision of the trier of fact at the close of a trial concerns the discharge of the legal burden of proof, and the judge so as to avoid grounds of appeal against a subsequent conviction must correctly sum up the incidence of the burden of proof.

Criminal cases

The general rule is: the prosecution bears the legal burden to prove all the elements of the offences they allege the defendant has committed. There is a presumption of innocence in favour of the defendant and the effect of this decision was to protect human rights. The rule was set out by Lord Sankey LC in *Woolmington v DPP* [1935] AC 462 he stated: '[In] English criminal law one golden thread is always seen, that is the duty of the prosecution to prove the prisoner's guilt subject to . . . insanity and . . . any statutory exception . . . this is part of the common law.'

Woolmington clarifies where the legal burden of proof lies in the prosecution of a criminal offence. If the prosecution fails to satisfy the evidential burden (fails to make a prima facie case) and therefore the legal burden of proof, then the defendant will be acquitted. It is of course the trier of fact that will decide, on conclusion of the trial, whether the burden has been discharged.

Exceptions

STATUTES IMPOSING A LEGAL AND EVIDENTIAL BURDEN

Figure 2.3 outlines examples of statutes that impose a legal burden of proof on the defendant:

Section 51(7) of the Criminal Justice and Public Order Act 1994 requires the defence to prove that the defendant lacked the relevant intention if they are charged with the offence of witness intimidation contrary to s 51(3).	Section 139(4) of the CJA 1988 requires the defence to prove that the defendant, where charged contrary to s 139, had good reason or lawful authority to be in possession of a bladed article in a public place.

Figure 2.3 Statutes imposing a legal burden of proof

Figure 2.4 sets out examples of statutes imposing an evidential burden of proof on the defendant:

Section 75(1) of the Sexual Offences Act 2003 in particular instances requires the defence to discharge an evidential burden that the alleged victim consented. The prosecution must then disprove that.	Sections 28(3) of the Misuse of Drugs Act 1971 imposes an evidential burden on the accused to prove that he or she lacked belief, suspicion or reason to suspect that they were in possession of a controlled substance.

Figure 2.4 Statutes imposing an evidential burden of proof

INSANITY

The defence of **insanity** is the only common law exception to the rule that the prosecution bears the legal burden of proof. If this defence is raised then the defence bears the legal burden to prove that the defendant was insane (see *M'Naghten's Case* (1843) 10 Cl & F 200). The judge should also distinguish the defence from automatism as the incidence of burden of proof varies (see *Bratty v AG for Northern Ireland* [1963] AC 386 *and R v Burns* [1973] 58 Cr App R 364). In light of advances in human rights law it is highly unlikely that a legal burden would now be placed on a defendant. In terms of other common law defences the defendant only bears an evidential burden.

EXPRESS STATUTORY EXCEPTIONS

There are a number of statutory provisions that place a legal burden on the defence; often this may be in relation to a specific element of an offence – this is known as a 'reverse' burden of proof. Lord Sankey LC referred to this in *Woolmington* (above). Section 2 of the Homicide Act 1957 is a good example of this which requires, in defence to a charge of murder, the defendant to prove that their responsibility was diminished.

IMPLIED STATUTORY EXCEPTIONS

Sometimes statute may imply a reverse burden. In summary trials, s 101 of the Magistrates' Courts Act 1980 provides that a defendant must prove any exception, exemption, proviso, excuse or qualification that they rely on in their defence, even where the complaint contains an allegation that negatives it (see *John v Humphreys* [1955] 1 WLR 325 and *Gatland v Metropolitan Police Commissioner* [1968] 2 QB 279).

R v Edwards [1975] QB 27 outlines the position in trials on indictment. In this case the Court of Appeal held that the common law contains a similar exception to the rule that the prosecution is required to prove the entirety of an offence. It applies to those offences that prohibit a particular act other than in certain circumstances, or by certain people (including those with permission). If the defendant seeks to rely on such a provision then they will bear the legal burden of proving that they fall within it. Additionally, Rule 6C of the Indictment Rules 1971 implies the legal burden of proof where an Act provides a defence by way of exception, exemption, proviso, excuse or qualification.

The implication of a legal burden on a defendant is a question for the court (statutory construction).

KEY CASE ANALYSIS: _R v Hunt_ [1987] AC 352

In this case the defendant was indicted on a charge for possession of morphine contrary to s 5 of the Misuse of Drugs Act 1971. Schedule 1 (paragraph 3) of the Act provided: s 5 had no effect where a preparation of morphine contained less than 0.2 percent morphine. Here the House of Lords held that the prosecution must prove that the preparation contained more than 0.2 percent morphine (which incidentally it had not); this was the proper construction of this Act.

This case is a good example of the fact that the resolution of a question on construction can be difficult to resolve.

Where an accused does bear the legal burden of proof, whether that is by reason of the common law of an Act of parliament, the standard to which they must discharge that is on the balance of probabilities (see _R v Carr-Briant_ [1943] KB 607). See also: _R v Webster_ [2010] EWCA 2819 where the Court of Appeal read down a reverse legal burden in the Prevention of Corruption Act 1916 as an evidential burden because it could not be justified as being compliant with the presumption of innocence.

On-the-spot question

 What is a reverse burden of proof?

HUMAN RIGHTS

Article 6(2) of the European Convention on Human Rights (ECHR) provides that everyone who is charged for the commission of a criminal offence will be presumed to be innocent until proven guilty. The issue this raises is whether a legal burden of proof placed on the defence can be compatible with the presumption of innocence. The House of Lords and Court of Appeal dealt with this in a number of cases. In *Attorney General's Reference (No.4 of 2002)* [2005] 1 AC 264 and *Sheldrake v DPP* [2004] UKHL 43 (consolidated appeals) the Lords held:

- An accused has an overriding right to a fair trial;
- The presumption of innocence is not absolute therefore derogation may be permitted but must be justified by the state;
- There must be a balance between individual rights and the broader interests of the European Community (European Union);
- The imposition of a reverse burden of proof must be justified as to why it is fair and reasonable to deny the accused the right afforded to everyone;
- When considering whether the imposition of a reverse burden is justified, the court should take into account:

  ○ The mischief (problem) that the provision that imposes the reverse burden aims to address;
  ○ The test to determine compatibility is 'reasonableness' and 'proportionality';
  ○ Issues of security do not justify a member state derogating from their duty to act in a fair manner;
  ○ The seriousness of the sentence that may result from conviction;
  ○ The nature and extent of the matters the accused must prove and how important they are when compared to those required to be proven by the prosecution;
  ○ Whether the matters are readily provable by the accused because they are within the accused's knowledge or to which they have ready access.

If an infringement cannot be justified the court will, if possible, 'read down' the provision under s 3 of the Human Rights Act 1998 (HRA). The effect of this is to impose an evidential rather than a legal burden on the accused (see *R v Lambert* [2002] 2 AC 545 and *Salabiaku v France* (1988) 13 EHRR 379); Section 3 compels the courts to interpret such provisions in a manner so that they are compatible with the ECHR, it states: 'So far as it is possible . . . primary legislation and subordinate legislation must be read and given effect in a way [that] is compatible with the Convention rights.'

Where this is not possible the court should, under s 4(2) of the HRA 1998, make a declaration of incompatibility. This seeks to initiate fast track change to the offending provision but as s 6(4) states: 'A declaration [of incompatibility] . . . does not affect the validity, [continued] operation or enforcement of [a] provision in respect of which it is given; and [it] is not binding on the parties to the proceedings in which it was made.'

On-the-spot question

 What is the effect of the HRA 1998 on placing the burden of proof on a defendant?

Civil cases

In civil cases the legal burden of proof is borne by the claimant. The Latin maxim *ei qui affirmat, non ei qui negat, incumbit probatio* applies (he who affirms, and not he who denies, must prove it). This is because it is the claimant who makes the claim and the defendant who must prove the opposite – which can be a far more difficult task (see *Joseph Constantine Steamship Line Ltd v Imperial Smelting Corporation Ltd* [1942] AC 154 – discussed below). In civil cases the parties are theoretically on an equal footing therefore, unlike criminal trials, there is no presumption that the party who brings the action bears the legal burden on every issue. For example, in a breach of contract the claimant will bear the legal burden of proving the contract existed, that it was breached and that subsequent loss occurred. If the defendant wishes to raise a defence, for instance frustration or mutual mistake or the valid incorporation of an exclusion clause (see *Levison v Patent Carpet Cleaning* [1977] 3 All ER 98), then they will bear the legal burden to prove that defence.

When deciding who is making the affirmative allegation, the substance of the issue must be considered and not simply how it seems to have been presented. The issue here lies with the use of a negative statement to describe a positive assertion, i.e. the defendant failed to do something rather than they allowed something to happen. In this instance the legal burden will still be borne by the claimant even though they have expressed an affirmative using a negative expression because they are still making the assertion.

On-the-spot question

 What is the general rule on burdens of proof in civil cases?

KEY CASE ANALYSIS: *Abrath v North Eastern Railway Company* **(1883) 11 QBD 440**

In this case a doctor issued a claim against the North Eastern Railway Company for a malicious prosecution after he was acquitted of a charge for conspiracy to defraud on the basis that he had colluded with the victim of an accident to exaggerate a claim. The doctor alleged the company had instituted proceedings against him 'without any reasonable or probable cause'. The court held that the burden was on the doctor to prove the malicious prosecution and the lack of reasonable or probable cause. The court held:

> ... [in] the assertion of a negative ... [the proposition was that when a negative is to be made out the onus shifts] ... This is not so. If the assertion of a negative is an essential part of the [claimant's claim] ... the proof of that assertion will still rest upon the [claimant]. The terms 'negative' and 'affirmative' are after all relative [but] not absolute.

The courts will consider a number of principles when considering who bears the legal burden of proof but, for all practical purposes, precedent and policy will determine this question. Whether a particular issue is 'essential to' that party's case depends on the substantive law; where a rule is not decisive the court will refer to the statements of claim and the **balance of convenience**.

KEY CASE ANALYSIS: *Joseph Constantine Steamship Line Ltd v Imperial Smelting Corporation Ltd* **[1942] AC 154**

Background

In this case the charterers of a steamship claimed damages resulting from an alleged breach of contract by the owners of that ship for a failure to load it by a particular date. The owner contended that the contract had been frustrated because the steamship had been destroyed by an explosion. The defence of frustration is raised in contract law where a breach may have resulted from an act that was not committed by fault of the defendant.

Principle established

The court held that the claimant bore the legal burden to prove the defendant was at fault. From the reasoning it is clear the court took the view that it would have been too onerous to require the defendant to prove a negative namely that it was not at fault.

KEY CASE ANALYSIS: *Levison v Patent Carpet Cleaning* [1977] 3 All ER 98

Background

In this case the contract for the cleaning of an expensive rug contained an exclusion clause for the defendant's liability in negligence. The company lost the rug and the claimant claimed a fundamental breach of contract (non-delivery) on the basis of negligence. The defendant claimed its liability was excluded by reason of the clause. The claimant contended that the defendant could not rely on the exclusion clause because the breach was a fundamental one.

Principle established

The Court of Appeal held, as per Lord Denning, that the defendant bore the legal burden to prove that the loss sustained by the claimant did not accrue by reason of a fundamental breach of contract by it. From the facts it is obvious that the claimant would have been put in an untenable position if required to prove the fundamental breach because she had no knowledge of what had actually happened to the carpet whereas the company would have.

You should note that in terms of exclusion clauses the claimant bears the legal burden to prove that the claim falls outside of it. For example if a clause provides that a party to the contract will not be liable for loss or damage to goods that occurs by seawater unless they are negligent, then a claimant bears the legal burden to prove the defendant was negligent (as per Lord Esher MR confirmed in *The Glendarroch* [1894] P 226, 231). Contrast this with *Munro, Brice and Company v War Risks Association* [1918] 2 KB 78 where the court held that the defendant must prove that their claim fell into a **proviso** to an exclusion clause.

Finally, the parties to a contract may lawfully agree a term that places the legal burden of proof on one of them in a particular instance provided it is clear. Section 13(1)(c) of the Unfair Contract Terms Act 1977 provides that for its purposes such a clause that changes the normal rules on where the burden lies is an exclusion clause.

On-the-spot question

In a civil case what factor determines who bears the burden of proof on an essential issue?

Evidential burden of proof

The evidential burden refers to the obligation to present evidence sufficient enough to raise an issue to the satisfaction of the trier of law; this will be the judge in a Crown Court trial. You should contrast this with the discharge of the legal burden that the jury will decide upon. It is often said that the party bearing the legal burden of proof has an onerous task because they must satisfy the evidential burden in order to raise an issue and then discharge the corresponding legal burden by persuading the tribunal of fact that what they allege is true. If the evidential burden is not discharged then that party will not have discharged the legal burden either. Where an evidential burden does not have a corresponding legal burden, for instance in the case of a defence, then if the accused fails to discharge the evidential burden the issue will not be put to the trier of fact. If the accused does discharge the evidential burden then the jury must decide whether the defence stands (see *R v Calvert* [2000] All ER (D) 2071).

The evidential burden may be distributed between the parties as the case proceeds. Essentially, the risk of an adverse finding shifts to the opposition when one side has discharged the evidential burden on an issue. For example, if the prosecution adduces evidence to support their case and therefore a submission of no case to answer is rejected, then the defendant is at risk of being found guilty. Thus, the defendant must adduce evidence to counter this. Often, it is not as simple as this for there are many issues to be tried in a criminal case and the evidence adduced by the prosecution in discharge of one issue may not be enough on its own to prove the defendant's guilt. You should note that as a matter of law the evidential burden does not shift on the issues in a trial, it is the risk that shifts.

Standards of proof

The term standard of proof refers to how far the triers of law and fact must be satisfied that the party has proven their case. It also refers to the quality of the evidence that the parties adduce in support of that which they contend. As discussed earlier, the party bearing an evidential burden is not required to produce evidence that is as persuasive as that produced by the party bearing the legal burden of proof. Where the defence produces evidence of equal quality to counter the allegations made by the prosecution then the defence will succeed. The quality of the evidence that the prosecution (criminal) or claimant (civil) is required to prove differs.

Criminal cases: standard of proof required to discharge the legal burden

The prosecution must discharge the legal burden by adducing evidence to the following standard of proof – the jury must be 'sure of guilt' or 'satisfied of guilt beyond reasonable doubt'.

Key Definition

In *R v Gray* (1973) 58 Cr App R 177 the direction for what amounts to a reasonable doubt appeared as follows:

> A reasonable doubt is that quality or kind of doubt, which, when you are dealing with matters of importance in your own affairs, you allow to influence you one way or another. (See also: *Walters v R* [1969] 2 AC 26).

This standard of proof is the highest that is found in law and its adoption is underpinned by policy reasons; the liberty of a potentially innocent person is at stake, an unsafe conviction is a miscarriage of justice but also very costly and time consuming. Beyond reasonable doubt is not the same as 'beyond the shadow of a doubt' nor 'on the balance of probabilities'. The latter is the standard of proof in civil proceedings and this is deemed as being too low for the purposes of rebutting the presumption of innocence. In *Miller v Minister of Pensions* [1947] 2 All ER 372 Lord Justice Denning confirmed that a criminal case must be proven beyond reasonable doubt and that nothing short of that would suffice.

Misdirection's by judges in terms of the standard required is often cause for appeal, for example using alternative terms such as 'satisfied' or 'certain' (see *R v Hepworth* (1955) 2 QB 600; *R v Law* (1961) Crim LR 52 and *R v Gray* (1974) 58 Cr App R 177). The only acceptable alternative is: 'satisfied so that you are sure' (see *R v Summers* (1952) 36 Cr App R 14).

Where an accused bears the legal burden of proof, for instance a statutory defence places the burden on them such as insanity, then the accused has to discharge that burden (prove the issue) so that the jury are satisfied on a balance of probabilities (see *R v Carr-Briant* [1943] KB 607).

On-the-spot questions

Is the term 'beyond reasonable doubt' clear?

In what instance would a defendant in a criminal case bear the legal burden of proof?

Civil cases: standard of proof required to discharge the legal burden

The standard of proof to discharge the legal burden in civil proceedings is on the balance of probabilities, for example the claimant must prove that their case is more probable than that of the defendant.

Key Definitions

Lord Justice Denning set out the definition of the term on the balance of probabilities in *Miller v Minister of Pensions* [1947] 2 All ER 372 as:

> ... [A] case must be proved on a reasonable degree of probability, but not so high as is required in a criminal case. If the evidence is such that the tribunal can say: 'we think it more probable than not' [then] the burden is discharged, but if the probabilities are equal it is not.

Where the issue in civil proceedings relates to an allegation that the other party has committed a crime, for instance fraud, the standard of proof to discharge the legal burden is still on the balance of probabilities (see *Hornal v Neuberger Products Ltd* [1957] 1 QB 247). Although you should note two points:

- There were many conflicting authorities on this issue and in any respect a criminal conviction can be used as best evidence in support of an issue in a civil trial.
- There is a compelling argument that the more serious the crime that is alleged the clearer the evidence in support should be (and *Re H (Minors)* [1996] AC 563 and *Re S-B (Children)* [2009] UKSC 17).

There are also a series of civil proceedings in which the standard of proof required is not on the balance of probabilities, examples of this are included in Figure 2.5 (below).

On-the-spot question

 How clear is the term 'on the balance of probabilities'?

Standard of proof	Proceedings
Beyond reasonable doubt	(a) to prove the contempt of a civil court (see Re Bramblevale Ltd [1970] Ch 128); and (b) the professional misconduct of a solicitor (see Re A Solicitor [1993] QB 69).
Strong, irrefragable evidence	in a claim for the rectification of a document (see *Roberts v Leicestershire County Council* [1961] Ch 555);
Clear and unequivocal evidence	to prove a change in domicile (see Re Fuld's Estate (No 3) [1968] P 675).

Figure 2.5 Alternative standards of proof in civil proceedings

Standard of proof required to discharge the evidential burden

In the criminal court whether the evidential burden has been discharged is a question of law determined by the judge. The party raising the issue should present evidence that is sufficient to persuade the judge to put the issue before the trier of fact; in the Crown Court this is the jury. There is no exact formula relating to the standard of proof that is required in order for the evidential burden to be discharged. A failure to discharge the burden will result in the issue not being put to the trier of fact.

On-the-spot question

What is the standard of proof required in both criminal and civil cases?

Standard of proof: summary

Figure 2.6 summarises the standard of proof required in a variety of circumstances:

Burden	Standard of proof
Criminal proceedings where the prosecution bears evidential and legal burden	The judge will decide whether the prosecution has discharged the evidential burden, namely that there is enough evidence to convince the trier of fact beyond reasonable doubt (see *R v Galbraith* [1981] 1 WLR 1039). The jury will decide whether the prosecution has achieved this standard.
Criminal proceedings where the accused bears evidential and legal burden of proof	For instance, in relation to a defence or where statute imposes a reverse burden of proof, the judge will decide whether the accused has discharged the evidential burden, namely that there is enough evidence to justify putting the issue to the trier of fact. The accused must discharge the legal burden by adducing evidence to convince the trier of fact on the balance of probabilities.
Criminal proceedings where the accused bears evidential burden only	For instance in relation to a defence, the accused must adduce evidence to raise a reasonable doubt in the mind of the judge in relation to their guilt (see *Bratty v AG for Northern Ireland* [1963] AC 386).
Civil proceedings where a party bears the evidential and legal burden of proof	To discharge the evidential and legal burden a party must adduce evidence that would satisfy the trier of law and fact on a balance of probabilities.
Civil proceedings where a defendant bears the evidential burden of proof only	To discharge the evidential burden the defendant must adduce enough evidence so as to equalise the evidence in the case, this leaves the trier of fact no choice but to rule in their favour because the party bearing the legal burden will not be able to discharge it.

Figure 2.6 Standard of proof in summary

SUMMARY

In criminal trials the existence of the presumption of innocence has strengthened the notion, with exceptions for instance in relation to certain defences, that the prosecution must prove every issue in a case against a defendant. A burden placed on a defendant must be read to be compatible with the HRA 1998. In civil cases the general rule is that the party who asserts an essential issue must prove it. The discussion of standards of proof has shown that even in civil cases the criminal standard of proof beyond reasonable doubt may operate.

FURTHER READING

Ashworth, A and Blake, M, 'The presumption of innocence in English Criminal Law' [1998] Crim LR 306.
This article discusses the presumption of innocence in English criminal law prior to the HRA 1998.

Denning, AT, 'Presumptions and Burdens' (1945) 61 LQR 379.
This is an article by the notorious Lord Denning; it explores the notion of the legal burden of proof.

Dennis, I, 'Reverse onuses and the presumption of innocence: In search of principle' [2005] Crim LR 901.
This article reviews the approach of the UK courts and relevant case law while exploring whether placing the burden of proof on a defendant is compatible with Art 6(2) of the ECHR.

Hamer, D, 'The presumption of innocence and reverse burdens: a balancing act' [2007] CLJ 66 142.
This article discusses the compatibility of the reverse burdens of proof with Article 6 of the ECHR.

Lewis, P, 'The Human Rights Act 1998: Shifting the burden' [2000] Crim LR 667.
This article discusses the compatibility of placing a legal burden of proof on a defendant and the presumption of innocence under the HRA 1998.

Phipson, S (2012). *Phipson on Evidence*. 17th edn. London: Sweet & Maxwell.
This is the practical authority on evidence in the United Kingdom; it examines, in detail, all aspects of the complex law. For burdens and standards of proof, see Chapter 4.

Williams, G, 'The evidential burden: Some common misapprehensions'. (1977) 127 NLJ 156.
This article explores a major discussion in evidence law, namely the nature, extent and the notion of the evidential burden on a defendant.

Chapter 3
Witness testimony

LEARNING OUTCOMES

By the end of this chapter, you should be able to:

- Critically engage with the legal principles relating to the oral evidence of witnesses
- Identify and distinguish between the instances in which witnesses may give sworn and unsworn evidence
- Determine the competence and compellability of a witness to give oral evidence
- Understand when special measures directions are available to assist particular types of witnesses to give oral evidence

INTRODUCTION

In this chapter the discussion will focus on **witness testimony** or the live oral evidence of a witness in court. This will include an exploration of rules on encouraging and compelling witnesses to give live evidence, when **sworn**, unsworn and **affirmed** evidence is given and the special measures that aid the young and the vulnerable to give live oral evidence.

WITNESS EVIDENCE AT COURT

The parties to a case, whether criminal or civil, will arrange for the court attendance of their witnesses. The oral evidence of a witness will be based predominantly on the statement they will have made prior to the trial although it should be noted that often witnesses deviate from their statement; hostile witnesses are discussed later in this chapter. The witness may refresh their memory from their witness statement prior to testifying and there is no rule of law prohibiting this. One of the purposes of a trial is to test the evidence admitted so as to ensure that any subsequent conviction is as safe as possible.

There are occasions when a witness may be **compellable** to give evidence but is unwilling, for whatever reason, to do so. Under s 97 of the Magistrates' Courts Act 1980 (MCA) and s 2 of the Criminal Procedure (Attendance of Witnesses) Act 1965 (CP(AW)A) that party may then apply to the court for an order that summons the witness to give evidence. The court will issue the summons if the witness concerned is likely to give 'material evidence' and where their attendance is necessary because it is in the **'interests of justice'**. Where that witness then fails to attend and they have no lawful excuse for doing so then attendance may be secured through arrest; the court may issue an arrest warrant so that they are detained and presented in court. If that witness then refuses to cooperate, for instance they refuse to answer the questions being put to them without lawful excuse, then they may be found to be in contempt of court, the penalty for which includes imprisonment, see *R v Adeojo (Sodiq)* [2013] EWCA Crim 41.

No party has any 'property' in a witness. In civil proceedings any contractual agreement giving one party exclusive right to a witness's evidence will be deemed void *ab initio* (see *Harmony Shipping Co v Saudi Europe Line Ltd* [1979] 1 WLR 1380). Therefore, witnesses are compellable for a claimant or defendant. In criminal proceedings a witness who has given evidence for the prosecution cannot then be called for the defence (*R v Kelly* (1985) *The Times*, 27th July).

THE PRESENTATION OF WITNESS EVIDENCE

First instance evidence is generally presented in the following order in criminal trials: the prosecution opens its case and then defence responds; in civil cases the claimant states their claim and then the defendant responds. On appeals it is the appellant and then the respondent; remember at this stage the respondent may be the original defendant or prosecution/claimant who had won at first instance but against whose win (on suitable grounds) the opposition is now appealing. The general rule is that the legal representative of the party will decide in which order they will call their evidence; this is always subject to any legal rules on this issue and, of course, basic logic. For instance the defendant, where they are giving evidence and there are more than two other defence witnesses, is required to testify first unless the court using its discretion decides otherwise (see s 79 the PACE Act 1984). You should note that there are instances in which the defendant may not testify and equally there are repercussions in this.

In civil and criminal trials witnesses are not permitted to remain in court prior to giving evidence; this is unless the judge makes an order to the contrary. The rationale that underpins the court excluding a witness until they have given evidence relates to preventing them being influenced by the evidence of other witnesses. In criminal trials there is no rule of law that excludes the evidence of a witness who remains in court while having been excluded until they had given evidence (see *R v Kingston* [1980] WLR 519). Although, the credibility of that witness and the weight ascribed to the evidence that they subsequently give will be called into question – these are matters for the court. Furthermore, in criminal cases witnesses may not discuss the case between themselves. Where witnesses breach this rule then the judge will consider the entirety of the circumstances including:

Figure 3.1 Witness evidence

KEY CASE ANALYSIS: *R v Shaw* [2002] EWCA Crim 3004

Shaw was charged with grievous bodily harm with intent. The victim had suffered serious injuries from the incident that resulted from road rage. Two independent witnesses were called to give evidence of the attacker's identity. During the course of the trial the witnesses discussed the case with one another and modified their evidence. The defence raised the issue and the judge directed the jury accordingly. Shaw was convicted and appealed. The Court of Appeal quashed his conviction because the fairness of the trial had been compromised. In coming to their decision the court took into account the fact that witnesses will often discuss the case, they may even know one another, but that the evidence of an independent witness should be uninfluenced – the witnesses should not try the defendant, that is the task of the jury.

Finally, once the prosecution has closed its case it will not be permitted to reopen it unless the trial judge, using their discretion, allows it; for example if:

- a matter arises after the prosecution has closed its case for instance the defence makes an allegation that the prosecution wishes to rebut;
- the prosecution fails to lead on its formal evidence (see *R v Francis* [1990] 1 WLR 1264 and *R v Jackson (Terry)* [1996] 2 Cr App R 420).

Additionally, the trial judge retains a residual discretion to allow evidence to be adduced to deal with any issues that may arise during the course of a trial (see *R v Munnery* (1990) 94 Cr App R 164). You should note that a trial judge should only use this discretion sparingly.

KEY CASE ANALYSIS: *R v Milliken* (1969) 53 Cr App R 330

The defendant was charged with possession of housebreaking implements by night. Two police officers gave evidence that they saw the accused in the doorway of an Old Bond Street building bent over the keyhole. There was considerable dispute in the evidence and cross-examination. The defence made an attack on the credibility and honesty of the police officers who were giving evidence. The trial judge allowed the prosecution to adduce evidence in rebuttal of this. (See also: *R v Rice* [1963] 1 QB 857).

SWORN, UNSWORN OR AFFIRMED EVIDENCE

The basic rule is as follows: the evidence of witnesses, other than children, in both criminal and civil cases must be sworn or affirmed. The requirement to give evidence on oath or affirmation is used to demonstrate that the witness understands the importance of giving truthful evidence and the solemnity of the occasion (dignified seriousness). Where the former is concerned, the oath is taken on the book sacred to the witness and this is clearly rooted in religion. In terms of the latter, often a witness will affirm not because they are atheist but because they believe it to be improper to use the text in such a way. In law there is no difference between the oath and the affirmation. Witnesses that lie on oath or affirmation are subject to the charge of perjury, which, if successfully proven, can result in a custodial sentence of up to seven years' imprisonment.

The procedure by which an oath may be taken is outlined by s 1 of the Oaths Act 1978 (OA). Section 1(3) of the OA allows the court to administer the oath in 'any lawful manner'. The court officer will normally ask the witness whether they would like to take the oath or affirm and, if the former, which text is sacred to them. The witness must then hold that text and, with the other hand held up, must state 'I swear by . . . that the evidence I shall give shall be the truth, the whole truth and nothing but the truth'. The wording is amended to refer to the tenets of the witness's religion. The oath will bind the witness if it appeared to the court that it bound their conscience and if the witness considered it to bind their conscience too. Thus, the administration of the oath in a lawful manner is not dependent upon the peculiarity of the religion (see *R v Chapman* [1980] Crim LR 42 and *R v Kemble* [1990] 3 All ER 116).

Instead of taking the oath the witness may choose to affirm instead; s 5 of the OA 1978 allows a witness to make a solemn affirmation where they refuse to take the oath or where taking the oath is not reasonably practicable at that time. For instance, in terms of the latter the court may not have access to the relevant sacred text. Other than children, the evidence of any witness who is unable to take the oath or affirm is not admissible in court.

Criminal cases

The rule that only sworn (or affirmed) evidence may be admitted in criminal cases is outlined in s 55(2)(b) of the Youth Justice and Criminal Evidence Act 1999, the Hayes test as discussed later in this chapter forms part of this; sufficient appreciation of the solemnity of the occasion, and the added responsibility to tell the truth. In addition, s 55(8) of the same statute outlines a test for intelligible testimony that the witness must satisfy before the evidence can be received by the court, this is; the witness need only understand the questions put to them and give answers that can be understood. Figure 3.2 outlines where the legal burden and standard of proof lie in relation to the competence of witnesses.

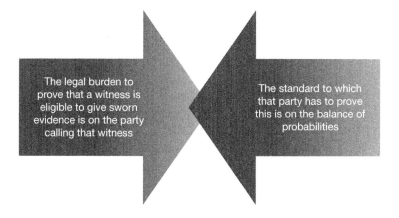

The legal burden to prove that a witness is eligible to give sworn evidence is on the party calling that witness

The standard to which that party has to prove this is on the balance of probabilities

Figure 3.2 Proof of witness eligibility to give sworn evidence

There are two points to note:

- where the witness is *under* the age of 14, they cannot give sworn (or affirmed) evidence. There is no statutory test that provides a witness the eligibility to give unsworn evidence; the evidence will be received by the court subject to the normal rules on relevance and admissibility; and
- where a witness *over* the age of 14 cannot satisfy the test in s 55(2)(b), then the court can receive their evidence unsworn.

COMPETENCE AND COMPELLABILITY

The **competence** of a witness to give evidence depends on whether the court can receive that evidence. Of course, the evidence may be relevant but not admissible and therefore the evidence would not be presented before the court in any event. Therefore, it can be stated that a witness's competence to give evidence depends on whether it is relevant and admissible (receivable by the court). A **competent** witness is also **compellable**, in other words they are obliged to give that evidence. Witnesses who, without lawful excuse, fail to give evidence, refuse to do so, or refuse to answer questions in court are liable to be tried for contempt of court. The following discussion focuses on the test for the competence of a variety of witness types (adults, spouses, children, accused or co-accused).

Competence in civil cases

In civil cases all witnesses are competent and compellable to give evidence by reason of the Evidence Act 1851, and the Evidence (Amendment) Act 1953 did the same in relation to the spouses of those parties. There are obvious exceptions to this, for example the mentally ill, sovereigns and diplomats – the former are discussed latter. The Evidence Act 1843 had originally abolished the rule that those with a conviction or with some interest in the outcome were incompetent to give evidence, for these matters can affect the weight that is attributed to the evidence itself (see also: *Omychund v Barker* (1744) 26 ER 15).

The test for competence, the '*Hayes test*' (see below) outlines the requirements for giving sworn evidence. Prior to this, in order to be sworn in as per the common law, an understanding of the oath also required the witness to have an appreciation of its connection with the grace of god (divine sanction, see *R v Brasier* (1779) 1 Leach 199). In deciding whether a witness is competent to give evidence the trial judge will consider whether (a) the witness appreciates the solemnity of the occasion and (b) they understand that taking the oath imposes on them an obligation to speak the truth over and above the ordinary duty to do so. The modern approach means that the witness does not have to be religiously inclined.

> **KEY CASE ANALYSIS:** *R v Hayes (Geoffrey)* [1977] 1 WLR 234
>
> Hayes was convicted of inciting three young boys, aged 12, 11 and 9, to commit acts of gross indecency. The judge, after questioning them, had allowed the youngest to give unsworn evidence and the two older ones to give sworn evidence, even though the eldest of them had said that although he was ignorant as to the existence of god he understood the importance of speaking the truth especially on this occasion. On an application for leave to appeal the issue before the court was whether the boys were competent to give sworn evidence. The court held (as per Lord Justice Bridge):
>
> > ... in the present state of society ... adult[s] [do not generally recognise the] ... divine sanction of an oath. The important consideration ... when a judge has to decide whether a child should properly be sworn in, is whether [that] child has a sufficient appreciation of the solemnity of the occasion, and the added responsibility to tell the truth ... involved in taking an oath, over and above the duty to tell the truth which is an ordinary duty of normal social conduct.

Children, anyone under the age of 18 (s 105 of the Children Act 1989 (CA)), are exceptions to the rule that witnesses must give sworn or affirmed evidence. Section 96(2) of the CA 1989 permits children to give unsworn evidence if they are incapable of being sworn in; the requirements are that:

- the child must understand their duty to speak the truth; and
- they must have sufficient understanding to justify their evidence being heard.

Competence in criminal cases

The credibility and reliability of witness evidence are not issues that concern the competence of a witness to give evidence; these matters will however affect the weight attached to the evidence that they give. Section 53(3) of the Youth Justice and Criminal Evidence Act 1999, which applies to all witnesses, imposes a two-stage test for witness competence to give evidence in criminal cases. The provision states that 'a person is not competent to give evidence in criminal proceedings if it appears to the court that [they] are unable to:

(a) understand questions put to [them] as a witness; and
(b) give answers to [those questions] that can be understood.'

The issue here is one of a witness understanding the questions put to them in court and giving answers that can be understood. Thus, only those who can communicate with others using a spoken language, for example English or French, are competent to give evidence in criminal proceedings, the latter through authorised court interpreters. Unlike the *Hayes test* the witness is not required to appreciate the difference between truth and untruth (*see R v MacPherson* [2006] EWCA Crim 3605). The trial judge will decide whether a witness is competent to give evidence after questioning them.

KEY CASE ANALYSIS: *R v M* [2008] EWCA 2751

This case concerned the testimony of a victim of sexual abuse, a young female aged nine with learning difficulties. The police interviewed her and a speech therapist was asked to assess the level of her disability; this was subsequently determined as being at a 'medium level'. At trial, the judge viewed the videoed evidence given by the victim to determine for himself the victim's competency to give evidence. In absence of the jury he ruled that she was not competent. The Crown Prosecution Service appealed the judge's decision that had prevented the jury from receiving the victim's evidence. The Court of Appeal stated in this case that it would very rarely interfere with a trial judge's decisions relating to competence.

For another example see: *DPP v R* [2007] EWHC 1842. Figure 3.3 outlines where the legal burden and standard of proof lie in relation to the competence of witnesses.

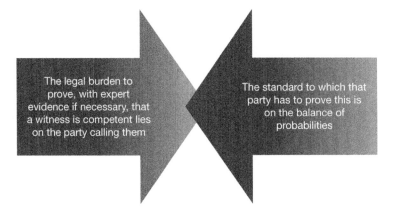

The legal burden to prove, with expert evidence if necessary, that a witness is competent lies on the party calling them

The standard to which that party has to prove this is on the balance of probabilities

Figure 3.3 Proof of witness competence

Section 54 of the Youth Justice and Criminal Evidence Act 1999 allows for relevant expert evidence to assist the court in this matter. The overall decision as to competence will lie with the trial judge; this exists throughout the entire trial. The effect of this is that a trial judge can rule that a witness is not competent to give evidence at any time. Therefore, a trial judge may rule that a witness is not competent to give evidence while they are in the process of giving oral testimony. In addition, the judge retains the power to exclude evidence under s 78 of the PACE Act 1984; this provision is discussed in Chapter 8.

There are a number of factors that the trial judge will consider when assessing the competence of a child to give testimony because of the time that will normally elapse between them having given their original statement and the trial itself. Although a time delay does preclude a court from hearing a child witness's evidence. In *R v B* [2010] EWCA 4 the Court of Appeal consolidated the authorities on this issue and gave the following guidance:

Point	Context
Confirmation that the test for competence laid down in s 53 of the Youth Justice and Criminal Evidence Act (YJCEA) 1999	The court clarified that this applies to all witnesses and that it does not require interpretation.
The provision requires the judge to form a judgement as to whether the witness satisfies the test	This serves to remove the criticism that the exercise of discretion carries with it – the consideration of arbitrary criteria as thought fit by the trial judge.
The test is to be applied to each witness independently	This avoids the consideration of irrelevant factors.
The witness need only understand the questions put to them and give answers that can be understood	The interpretation makes the test less onerous to satisfy, the witness need not understand the importance to tell the truth, all the questions put to them or answer every question.
Age is not a condition that prevents anyone giving accurate and honest evidence	This makes the point that witness credibility is a matter for the trier of fact to form a judgement on themselves.
Competency may be reconsidered once the child witness has finished giving their testimony	The court has taken into account the practice of trial judges in various cases on this matter. This also allows the trial judge the ability to change their mind having seen the witness giving evidence; not to allow this would be an affront to common sense.

Figure 3.4 Witness competency test

Figure 3.5 outlines the series of complex rules that relate to the competence and compellability of various witnesses to give evidence, for example the defendant and his or her spouse or an accomplice who is jointly charged with the crime.

Witness	Rules
Defendant	Section 53(1) of the YJCEA 1999 states all persons, regardless of age, are competent to give evidence in criminal proceedings. Section 53(4) provides that a person charged, whether solely or otherwise, in criminal proceedings is not competent to give evidence for the Crown. Section 53(5) defines a person charged as being on trial, whether summarily or on indictment, after having pleaded not guilty to the allegation. By reason of the common law a defendant is not compellable to testify for him- or herself or others including the prosecution because they had an interest in the proceedings. They are also protected by the privilege against self-incrimination (see Chapter 5) and there are limits to this, for instance the effect of remaining silent can result in negative inferences being drawn under the Criminal Justice and Public Order Act 1994 (see Chapter 6).
Accomplices	The prosecution can call an alleged accomplice as a witness in three ways: By entering a *nolle prosequi* against them, this means that they are unwilling to proceed with the prosecution against them (see s 67 of the CJA 1967). The person is then treated as any other witness: they will be competent and compellable for the prosecution. Where a separate trial is ordered against the accomplice: this may be to save time but often it rests on the parties being able to present a fuller picture of the entire event to a jury. You should note that where separate trials are ordered the jury can often return different verdicts, see *R v Moghul* (1977) 65 Cr App R 56. If the accomplice pleads guilty to the allegation they will no longer fall under the definition of a person charged with a criminal offence (see s 53(5) of the YJCEA 1999). The accomplice will be sentenced or sentencing will be delayed until the conclusion of the co-accused's trial; this is to prevent the accomplice manipulating their evidence so as to affect the sentence they receive. The person will then be treated as any other witness and will be both competent and compellable for the prosecution.

Figure 3.5 Witness competency

Witness	Rules
Defendant's spouse/civil partner	By reason of the common law a defendant's spouse or civil partner (CP) was not compellable to testify in civil and criminal proceedings because they too had an interest in the proceedings. Various statutory provisions have reduced the application of this rule in the modern day. Spouses/CPs are competent to testify provided they are not a person charged themselves (see: s 80(1) and s 80(4) of the PACE Act 1984 and s 53(3) of the YJCEA 1999).
Defendant's spouse/civil partner for accomplices or the prosecution	Sections 80(2) and 80(3) of the PACE Act 1984 provide that the spouse or CP is competent and compellable to give evidence on behalf of accomplices or prosecution in relation to a specified offence whether they are a witness or the victim. The latter must *involve*: • an assault on, or injury or a threat of injury to, the spouse or civil partner or a person who was at the material time under the age of 16; • a sexual offence alleged to have been committed in respect of a person who was at the material time under that age; or • attempting or conspiring to commit, or of aiding, abetting, counselling, procuring or inciting the commission of, an offence falling within the previous two. The fact that the witness is compellable is in the public interest. The section also states that ex-partners and those divorced, are competent and compellable to give evidence as though they had never entered into that lawful arrangement. The provisions do not apply where the spouse is co-accused. The trial judge may choose to inform (warn) the spouse of an accused who does not fall into this above law and is therefore not compellable to give evidence for the prosecution but chooses to do so that they cannot be compelled to give that evidence (see *R v Acaster* (1912) 106 LT 384). The judge is not obliged, as a rule of law, to give that warning (see *R v Pitt* [1982] 3 WLR 359). Finally, the prosecution, but not a trial judge in limited circumstances, is prohibited from commenting on the failure of the spouse to give evidence (s 80A the PACE Act 1984 and *R v Naudeer* [1984] 3 All ER 1036, CA).

Figure 3.5 *continued*

On-the-spot question

 In what instance may a co-accused give evidence on behalf of the prosecution?

OTHER FACTORS RELATING TO WITNESSES

The remaining discussion focuses on the variety of other factors that may affect the ability of a witness to give evidence, for example fear and mental capacity.

Special measures orders

The YJCEA 1999 allows a trial judge to make special measures directions in criminal proceedings. These are designed to support a witness who is disabled, intimidated, young or vulnerable in giving evidence. Part 29 of the current Criminal Procedure Rules (2005) outlines the procedure that must be followed (see further reading at the end of the chapter for the web link). The direction may: allow a witness to give evidence via **live link** (video conference, see ss 33A and B); screen the witness from the accused; require lawyers to remove their wigs and gowns; allow a special device that may aid their communication; allow examination-in-chief to take place in private (in-camera) or through an intermediary; or to allow a video recording to stand as the witness's examination-in-chief, cross-examination and re-examination. Figure 3.6 summarises what type of witnesses are eligible to apply for this support:

Although the defence or prosecution may apply for a special measures direction, the court may make one of its own volition (see s 19 of the YJCEA 1999). The question for the court, having regard to all the circumstances, is whether any of the directions would support the witness in giving better evidence. The court can choose to grant, discharge, refuse to grant

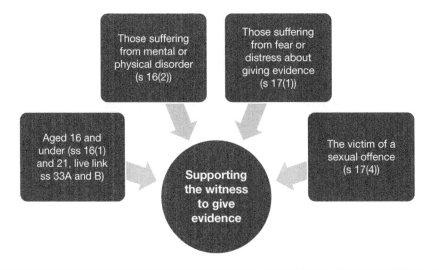

Figure 3.6 Special measures directions

or vary a special measures direction – but each of these decisions must be stated by it in open court. You should note that:

- Video recorded evidence and evidence by live link are mandatory where witnesses are under the age of 16 (s 21).
- Witnesses who are aged 18 at the time of trial but were under that age at the time their evidence was recorded are still covered by the provisions (ss 21 and 22).
- The trial judge must give the jury a warning, as he or she considers necessary, to ensure that the direction that was given in relation to a particular witness does not prejudice the accused (s 32).
- The evidence will carry the same weight it would have had it been given in open court.

On-the-spot question

What do you think was parliament's intention when introducing special measures?

The Ministry of Justice (United Kingdom) has produced guidance for achieving best evidence by using special measures in criminal proceedings (see further reading for the web link). Access to special measures is for the court to determine using the following three tests:

Test One Is the witness either vulnerable or intimidated as required by ss 16 and 17 of the YJCEA 1999?

Test Two Will any of the special measures taken alone or in combination improve the quality (accuracy, completeness and coherence) of the witness's evidence? The court must take into account the view of the witness and the possibility that the special measures may limit the extent to which the evidence can be tested.

Test Three Which, if any, of the special measures is likely to maximise the quality of the witness's evidence?

Figure 3.7 Tests for special measures

Therefore, it does not automatically follow that a witness who is eligible to be supported by a special measures direction will be given that support. The court must take into account the 'interests of justice' when it is considering the admission of video recorded evidence.

Witnesses of defective intellect

The competency of an individual that falls under this category to give evidence is determined by s 53 of the YJCEA 1999 as discussed earlier in the chapter (see also: *R v McKenzie* [1992] *The Independent*, 28 July and *Boughton v Knight* (1873) LR 3 P&M 64).

Special witnesses: diplomats and heads of state

Such witnesses are competent to give evidence but cannot be compelled to do so in either civil nor criminal trials.

Anonymity

Section 86(1) in Chapter 2 of the Coroners and Justice Act 2009 (C&JA) provides that if a court considers it appropriate it may grant a witness anonymity order in criminal trials to ensure that the identity of the witness is not disclosed in or in connection with the proceedings. The order can cover, among other things, withholding the witness's name and other identifying details, using a pseudonym and modulating (electronically modifying) the witness's voice to prevent recognition. An application for a witness anonymity order can be made by the prosecution or the defence. Section 88 provides that the court can only make the order if:

- the order is necessary to protect the safety of the witness or another person, or to prevent serious damage to property, prevent real harm to the public interest (the carrying on of activities in the public interest or the safety of the person carrying on the activities in the public interest);
- after having considered all the circumstances, the effect of the order would be consistent with the defendant receiving a fair trial; and
- the importance of the witness's testimony is such that it is in the interests of justice that they testify and the witness would not testify unless the order is made or there would be real harm to the public interest if the witness testified without the order being made.

The court will take into account, among other things, the right of the defendant to know the identity of the witness, the credibility of the witness and whether it is reasonably practicable to protect the witness by any other means (see s 89 of the C&JA 2009). Finally, in a trial on indictment where a witness anonymity order has been in place the trial judge must give to the jury, as he or she considers appropriate, such warning to ensure the fact that the order was made does not prejudice the defendant (s 90).

Witness familiarisation and training

Witnesses, regardless of whether they are vulnerable or intimated, will require support prior to giving evidence. They will need information as to their role and assistance to ensure that they give their best evidence. Such support does not include discussing or rehearsing their evidence with them or coaching them before trial – 'training' witnesses prior to trial is prohibited. The rules do not prohibit witness familiarisation visits provided that the guidance given in relation to these is followed. In short, the witness can be shown the facilities (courtroom or live link room) but a discussion of their evidence is strictly prohibited (*R v Momodou & Limani* [2005] EWCA Crim 177).

SUMMARY

The term competence refers to the *ability* of a witness to give evidence and compellability is the *requirement* to do so. The statutory test for competence in criminal cases is provided by s 53 of the YJCEA 1999 and in civil cases competence is determined by the *Hayes test*. The general common law rule is that all competent witnesses are compellable, with obvious exceptions, in criminal proceedings. The court may support the witness's ability to give their best evidence through special measures directions, witness anonymity orders and familiarisation.

FURTHER READING

Achieving Best Evidence in Criminal Proceedings: Guidance on interviewing victims and witnesses, and guidance on using special measures. March 2011, MOJ.

Available at: www.justice.gov.uk/downloads/victims-and-witnesses/vulnerable-witnesses/achieving-best-evidence-criminal-proceedings.pdf.
This booklet was issued by the Ministry of Justice to provide guidance to practitioners on aiding a witness to give best evidence. The guide is comprehensive and includes information of witness familiarisation as well as special measures.

Brammer, A and Cooper, P, 'Still waiting for a meeting of minds: child witnesses in the criminal and family justice systems' [2011] 12 Crim LR 925.
This article focuses on the developments in the law and practice in criminal courts in relation to child witnesses and compares them with the approach taken by the family courts.

Creighton, P, 'Spouse competence and compellability' [1990] Crim LR 34.
This article explores the rules on the competence and compellability of spouses in criminal proceedings.

Keane, A, 'The Use at Trial of Scientific Findings relating to Human Memory' [2010] 1 Crim LR 19.
This article explores the guidelines on memory and the law; a report by the Research Board of the British Psychological Society.

Part 29 of the Criminal Procedure Rules (2005).
Available at: www.legislation.gov.uk/uksi/2005/384/part/29/made.
This part of the rules sets out the rules in relation to special measures, for instance the protocols and applications procedure that must be followed.

Wurtzel, D, 'It's all about best evidence', 2007, August 8–10, *Counsel: Journal of the Bar of England*. London: Taylor & Francis.
In this article the author discusses the rights of vulnerable witnesses to give best evidence.

Chapter 4
Witness evidence: The trial process

LEARNING OUTCOMES

By the end of this chapter, you should be able to:

- Critically engage with the principles relating to witness evidence during the trial process
- Understand the distinction between evidence-in-chief, cross-examination and re-examination and their functions
- Determine the rules that apply when treating witnesses as hostile or unfavourable during a trial and their purpose and effect
- Explore the notion of credibility and previous statements and their impact on witness evidence

INTRODUCTION

In this chapter the discussion will focus on witness testimony in the **trial process**. This will include an exploration of the rules that apply in eliciting witness evidence-in-chief, cross-examination and re-examination, when a witness turns **hostile** or **unfavourable** and issues of witness **credibility**. We will also discuss previous consistent and inconsistent witness statements and the principles governing witnesses refreshing their memory from documents.

WITNESS TESTIMONY

Chapters 1–3 highlighted the variety of rules that exist in relation to getting the evidence to court, for instance admissibility, relevance, the burden of proof and witness competence and compellability. The discussion in this chapter will focus on the principles that apply in relation to the presentation of that evidence in court during the trial process.

The stages of giving evidence

Once the witness has taken the oath or affirmed, or where the judge has permitted that witness to give unsworn evidence, the witness can begin to give evidence. Contrary to the belief of many, the witness is not given the permission to tell their story of their own accord. The witness will be guided through the process of them giving evidence by the party calling them or their legal representatives (barristers and solicitors). Under no circumstances does this mean that the advocates elicit untruths. The process aids the witness to give their best evidence and for the court to receive and test the same in the most efficient and effective way. You should note, as discussed in Chapter 3, the Court of Appeal highlighted that witness coaching is strictly prohibited and distinguished this from lawyers lawfully training or familiarising a witness with the court (see *R v Momodou* [2005] EWCA Crim 177, particularly paragraphs 61–65 of the judgment and *Ultraframe (UK) Ltd v Fielding & Others* [2005] EWHC 1638). Coaching a witness is unlawful because it affects the evidence that they give, which can lead to unlawful convictions and miscarriages of justice. In light of this the Bar Standards Board – the authority that regulates the practice of barristers in England and Wales – issued guidance to advocates on how to familiarise witnesses on court attendance without falling foul of the rules (see further reading, at the end of this chapter). The process of eliciting and testing the evidence (court advocacy) has three stages:

- examination-in-chief
- cross-examination
- re-examination.

There are quite strict rules in relation to all three stages, Figure 4.1 summarises these.

The following discussion explores each of these in more depth.

Examination-in-chief

This stage in the process of giving evidence, also known as direct examination, involves the witness taking to the witness box and the party calling them eliciting evidence that supports their case. The evidence will be relevant to the facts in issue and must be from the witness's personal knowledge: things they heard, saw or perceived. There are a number of rules and statutory provisions that relate to hearsay and opinion evidence that are discussed later in Chapter 7. The witness must not draw inferences, for that is the function of the jury. For example, if a witness (X) saw Y (the victim) with a black eye and bleeding nose they must not infer from that Y has been in a fight; that will be for the jury to conclude if it so chooses. However, it is not unusual for the witness to be asked what they had concluded and the reason for that. For instance X could state that Y's injuries gave the impression that they had just been attacked. Examination-in-chief will allow counsel to take the witness to the most salient points. Generally, the court will not allow an expert to give evidence as to a witness's credibility – there are exceptions to this, for instance the use of experts where a witness has a mental health issue or a learning difficulty.

While in the course of being examined-in-chief a witness might need to refresh his or her memory of the facts that they witnessed. This is usually because of the amount of time that

Stage	Purpose by party and rule(s)
Examination-in-chief	Prosecution: to elicit the evidence that supports the facts in issue (allegations). Defence: to elicit the evidence that undermines the facts in issue (allegations) and raises any potential defences. Neither of the parties may ask leading questions, for example: You clearly saw the defendant didn't you? However, the lawyers may, through appropriate questioning, guide the witness to elicit best evidence, for example: Can you describe to the court in your own words what happened that evening? When you saw the defendant running towards you with the bloodied knife, what did you do? Note: the latter of these adopts the narrative given by the witness and therefore does not fall foul of the rule that the advocate must not end up giving the evidence him- or herself. The trial judge has the discretion to allow leading questions if it is in the interests of justice to do so; this discretion cannot be questioned.
Cross-examination	Prosecution: to undermine the evidence presented by the defence witness and elicit evidence favourable to the prosecution. Defence: to undermine the evidence presented by the prosecution witness and elicit evidence favourable to the defence. Both prosecution and defence may lead the witness at this stage. Common questions will include: It all happened so fast that you didn't actually see very much did you? The purpose of this stage is to discredit the evidence presented by the witness.
Re-examination	Prosecution and defence: to mitigate the effect of the cross-examination on the witness's evidence, and deal with any new matters that arose. For instance, the defence might have raised the point that the witness's identification was impeded by their poor eyesight and conditions of lighting at the time. The prosecution can counter this by highlighting, through non-leading questions, that the witness actually saw the defendant from a close proximity under a streetlight.

Figure 4.1 Stages in giving evidence

has elapsed between the commission of the offence and the actual trial. The time limits within which an accused must be brought before a court are proscribed under the PACE Act 1984; for the purposes of this discussion an accused can remain in custody for up to 180 days (six months) before being brought to the Crown Court for a trial.The purpose of the trial is to test the evidence so as to secure a **safe conviction**. Thus, at common law, a witness is entitled to refresh his or her memory at any time before and during the trial process – the application of the rules varies depending upon the stage at which the witness wishes to refresh his or her memory, this issue is further discussed later in this section.

In certain instances, for example the evidence of the young and vulnerable, the court may permit that witness to give their evidence by video or live link (video conference) as a special measure (see Chapter 3). The basic rule at this stage is that the advocate must not ask leading questions on facts in dispute; this allows the witness to give evidence in their own words. Leading questions are designed to prompt the witness to give a particular answer; these types of questions assume that particular facts (usually those in dispute) exist. However, this does not mean that the advocate cannot guide the witness to the salient points through his or her questioning. There are many issues that can arise where a witness 'runs away with themselves' while giving evidence, for instance they may give an opinion on something they are not qualified to comment on, or they may attack the credibility of a defendant and therefore lose protection from being questioned on their own shady past. While this is not a book on advocacy, a perusal through one will provide some context to this chapter (see further reading, for details). The opposition will normally 'object' to a leading question, the trial judge would then decide whether the objection is 'overruled' (unfounded) or 'sustained' (made out). The answer to the leading question does not become inadmissible but the weight attached to it is affected (see the contrary but incorrect view in *R v Wilson* (*alias Whittingdale*) (1913) 9 Cr App R 124). Leading questions on undisputed facts do not pose the same issue. You should also bear in mind that the trial judge can waive the requirement for a witness to be examined-in-chief by a special measures order under s 27 of the Youth Justice and Public Order Act 1994 (YJPOA) (see Chapter 3).

If a witness dies before their evidence can be tested by cross-examination then their testimony will still stand as good evidence, although the weight attached to it will be significantly less. In this instance, in criminal cases the trial judge has the choice of discharging the jury or continuing with the trial and giving the jury appropriate warnings when **summing up**.

On-the-spot question

 What is the purpose of examination-in-chief?

Cross-examination

The counterpart to examination-in-chief is cross-examination. The opposition has the right to cross-examine a witness who has been called to give evidence even if the witness's examination-in-chief is waived or counsel decides not to ask them any questions. In *Creevy v Carr* (1835) 7 C & P 64 the trial judge stopped a witness during his examination-in-chief before any material question was posed to him, the witness was therefore not open to be cross-examined as clearly that would be a waste of the court's time. At this stage of the proceedings witnesses may be asked leading questions and they are compellable to answer the questions that are put to them unless they are protected by public policy or privilege – these are discussed later in Chapter 5. Permissible cross-examination will relate to the facts in issue and the credibility of the witness. The purpose of cross-examination is to destroy, qualify or weaken the evidence of a witness and thereby establish, through the opponent's witnesses, your own case. For example, in a case bearing on eyewitness evidence, the witness may be questioned about their account – perhaps the identification took place late at night in an unlit street. The cross-examiner is not confined to matters that are proven during examination-in-chief and may end up eliciting direct evidence that undermines the witness's account. Tactically, the prosecution may even cross-examine a defendant as a means of obtaining evidence against any co-accused.

The rules in cross-examination permit counsel for the opposition to ask leading questions and can therefore directly contradict the witness. Where contradictions exist between the versions given by witnesses, then counsel for the opposition can question them in relation to the evidence that other witnesses have given; this serves to outline the inconsistencies between the versions and highlight that the witnesses disagree as to the actual version of the events, which undermines the evidence. In *R v Flynn* [1972] Crim LR 428 the court made it clear that witnesses are entitled to consideration and courtesy during cross-examination in court and therefore irrelevant or unsupported criminal accusation will be deemed unreasonable, not to mention a waste of the courts resource. Furthermore, trial judges will, especially in cases involving sexual offences, aim to minimise any further trauma to the victim witness(es) during cross-examination. The special measures provided to help elicit best evidence from vulnerable witnesses under s 28 of the YJCEA 1999 are a good example of this. You should note that there are parts of this latter provision that are not yet in force. Generally, the party calling a witness may not cross-examine them (see *Re Woodfine* (1878) 26 WR 678) unless the witness becomes **hostile** or **adverse**. In this instance the trial judge may exercise their common law discretion and permit counsel to cross-examine them; Figure 4.2 (below) summarises the rules.

A witness can become hostile before being called to give evidence, during examination-in-chief, cross-examination and even re-examination (see *R v Powell* [1985] Crim L R 592). The purpose of treating a witness as hostile is to either contradict their evidence or bring them back into accordance with their original testimony; the latter is fairly unlikely in such situations. Section 3 of the Criminal Procedure Act 1865 (CPA), which applies in both

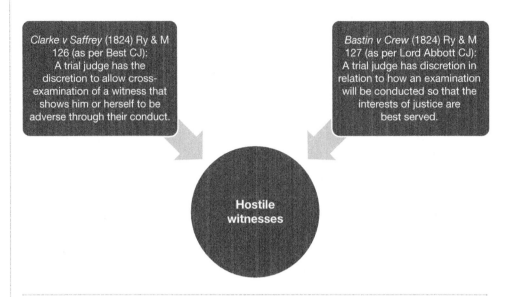

Figure 4.2 Common law discretion: hostile or adverse witnesses

criminal and civil proceedings, supplemented the principles of the common law. The provision prohibits a party producing (bringing forth) a witness to then discredit them but they may, with the leave of the judge, contradict them where they prove to be adverse. The witness may have made an inconsistent statement or changed their statement while giving testimony. Counsel may seek to contradict them through a previous statement they may have made or through the evidence of other witnesses (see *Greenough v Eccles* (1859) 28 JCP 160).

If the witness denies making the statement then s 4 of the CPA 1865 allows proof of the statement to be given after the 'circumstances of the supposed statement sufficient to designate the occasion' are mentioned to the witness and they are specifically questioned on whether they made the statement. Section 5 of the CPA 1865 allows a witness to be cross-examined as to previous statements made by him or her in writing or that were reduced to written form without the need for the statement to be shown to them – albeit counsel cross-examining must have the document available to them (see *R v Anderson* (1929) 21 Cr App R 178). The witness has no right to demand to see the written statement before they answer the question (see *Sladden v Sergeant* (1858) 175 ER 746). Under this provision, if the purpose of the cross-examination is to contradict the witness, they must be first questioned on those parts of the statement that will later be used in contradiction and then the contradictory statements must be read out in court so as to include them as part of the evidence. If counsel does not read out the contradictory statement they will be bound by the answer the witness has given, i.e. there will be no contradiction. The trial judge retains the discretion to require counsel to produce the statement for his or her inspection.

The Court of Appeal in *R v Thompson* (1977) 64 Cr App R 96 confirmed that these statutory provisions had not affected the judge's common law discretion. Furthermore, there is no difference between the terms hostile and adverse; what is required is that the witness becomes hostile or adverse to the party calling them by effectively 'changing sides' and therefore not giving evidence fairly (see *Greenough v Eccles* (1858) 141 CR 315). This will also call the truthfulness of the witness into question. However, a witness will not be adverse under the statute if their evidence is merely unfavourable, for example the party is not satisfied with the witness's performance because they do not come up to proof or where the witness's testimony contradicts the argument seeking to establish the facts in issue. In establishing that the witness is adverse, under the statute, the trial judge will pose two questions and these are:

* Has the witness proven to be adverse?
* If yes, then should leave to cross-examine the witness on the statement be granted?

In addition, proof of the original statement may be required (see *R v Booth* [1981] Crim LR 700). The evidential status of the statement was governed by the common law; the previous inconsistent statement did not become evidence of the facts it contained but was only relevant to the witness's credibility (see *R v Golder and Others* (1960) 45 Cr App R 5). The current position in criminal proceedings is similar to that in civil proceedings. Thus, a previous inconsistent statement made by a hostile witness will become their testimony where they accept it either because they admit making it or it is proven under ss 3–5 of the CPA 1865 (see also the s 119 of the CJA 2003). The statement will be admissible as evidence of any matter stated therein if oral evidence in relation to that same matter would have been admissible, and it will also be admissible as evidence of the truth of the facts it contains. In summing up, the trial judge can lawfully direct the jury that they may choose whether to rely on the witness's testimony or the previous inconsistent statement (see *R v Joyce* [2005] EWCA Crim 1785).

Finally s 6(3) of the Civil Evidence Act 1995 states that evidence of a previous inconsistent statement may only be adduced in line with s 3 of the CPA 1865.

KEY CASE ANALYSIS: *R v Norton and Driver (No. 1)* [1987] Crim LR 687 (CA)

Background

The appellants had been convicted of making off without payment. During examination-in-chief, a witness for the prosecution repeatedly stated that he could not remember what had happened. However, during cross-examination he suddenly remembered everything and gave evidence that cleared the appellants. The prosecution applied to the judge to treat the witness as hostile; the judge permitted this for purposes of re-examination. Relying on the decision in *R v Powell* [1985] Crim L R 592 the Court of Appeal decided that the prosecution was permitted to do so, as s 3 of the CPA 1865 did not differentiate between hostility that arose during examination-in-chief, cross-examination or re-examination.

Principle established

The principle from this case confirms that 'producing' (bringing forth) a witness, as per the words of the statutory provision, is a continuing act that does not stop once the witness has been examined-in-chief. Additionally, the application to treat the witness as hostile must be made to the trial judge as soon as the party identifies them as being so.

On-the-spot question

Think of an example in which a witness may be deemed as being hostile to the interests of the party calling them.

COLLATERAL MATTERS AND FINALITY OF ANSWERS RULE

The party cross-examining a witness is generally prohibited from calling witnesses that contradict or impeach that witness in terms of credit or other collateral matters; it is considered that the witness's answer will be final. Collateral matters are not directly related to a fact in issue and can distract the attention of the jury from the matters in dispute. For example, Mary is a witness to a theft from a shop; she is questioned by counsel in relation to her selling counterfeit goods two years ago. If Mary denies this then counsel cannot produce another witness to show that Mary is not telling the truth nor may they produce the counterfeit goods themselves. In absence of a conviction for the offence the witness cannot be contradicted by other evidence in relation to the same.

Therefore, counsel wishing to contradict a witness on a matter will have to determine whether it is in fact a collateral matter or if it is connected with the facts in issue (the dispute). To do so they will have to satisfy this test: is the witness's answer a matter in relation to which you can adduce evidence of your own right and has it got such a connection with the issues that you would be allowed to give evidence in relation to it? If the answer is yes, then that is a matter on which the witness can be contradicted because it is not a collateral matter (see *AG v Hitchcock* (1847) 1 Exch 91 as per Pollock CB). The rationale behind this is quite clear: by identifying what does not amount to a collateral matter the rule operates to prevent trials becoming unduly lengthy and overly complex through what could be a never-ending battle between competing legal interests.

KEY CASE ANALYSIS: *AG v Hitchcock* (1847) 1 Exch 91

Background

The defendant was accused of making whisky in a cistern without having a licence. In cross-examination a prosecution witness (A) was asked if he had told B that he had been offered a sum of money to say that the cistern had been used for this purpose. A denied ever having made the statement.

Principle established

Counsel for the defence wished to call B as a witness but the trials judge refused to allow this on the basis that the witness's answer was final. In short, A's answer was collateral to the fact in issue; it was irrelevant as to the unlawful use of the cistern.

There are also a number of exceptions to the rule. In both civil and criminal cases s 6 of the CPA 1865 allows counsel, without the leave of the trial judge, to adduce evidence to prove that a witness has been previously convicted of an offence where the witness during cross-examination denies, refuses to admit or does not answer a question relating to his or her antecedents (convictions) history (see also ss 100–101 of the CJA 2003). The witness should not be questioned in relation to convictions that are 'spent' under the Rehabilitation of Offenders Act 1974 (ROA) unless it is required 'in the interests of justice' and that is a matter for the trial judge to determine (see s 7(3) of the ROA 1974).

Again, in both civil and criminal proceedings, witnesses may be cross-examined to expose their bias or partiality in regard to a particular issue or person, therefore a denial by the witness may be rebutted through evidence that seeks to discredit them. Furthermore, counsel may lawfully adduce witness evidence to show, from the witness's personal knowledge, that the evidence of an opposing witness should not be believed or that they have a reputation for being untruthful – both these will seek to discredit the witness. You should note that, in terms of the latter, the witness giving this evidence need not show that his or her belief is based on their personal knowledge (see *R v Richardson and Longman* [1969] 1 QB 299). Finally, counsel may also lawfully adduce witness evidence to show, from the witness's personal knowledge, that the truthfulness of the opposition witness is affected by a physical or mental disability they are (or were) suffering, for instance the witness is registered deaf and without their hearing aid they could not have heard what they are suggesting they heard (see *Toohey v Metropolitan Police Commissioner* [1965] AC 595).

RE-EXAMINATION

In *The Queens Case* (1820) 2 Br & B 284 it was confirmed that the right to re-examine a witness only exists when they have (a) been examined-in-chief and (b) cross-examined. Furthermore, re-examination is strictly restricted to only those matters that arose while the witness was being cross-examined. Figure 4.3 summarises the position (below).

The purpose of re-examination is not to allow the party calling the witness to cross-examine them, to ask them leading questions, elicit further explanations on facts in relation to which evidence has already been given nor elicit any new facts. Although, in terms of the latter, the trial judge may grant leave for new facts to be elicited, for example counsel may wish to adduce a previous consistent statement in rebuttal of an allegation made in cross-examination that the witness has recently fabricated their testimony. The trial judge may elicit new facts by posing a question that achieves this him- or herself; in this instance counsel in opposition may cross-examine the witness on those facts. Therefore, in re-examination the witness may give an explanation for an answer given in cross-examination – the purpose being to highlight those points most favourable to the party's case and limit any damage to credibility. This entire process aims to 'test' the evidence.

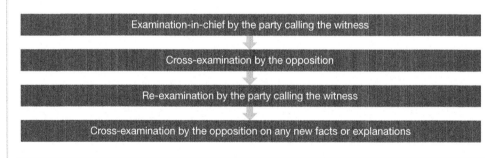

Figure 4.3 Testing the evidence

On-the-spot question

 Summarise how re-examination differs from cross-examination.

QUESTIONS BY THE JUDGE IN THE INTERESTS OF JUSTICE AND JURY

The trial judge may, in the interests of justice, pose any questions to witnesses including questions on those matters that he or she has **judicially noted**. In so doing the trial judge must be cautious not to suggest that he or she is satisfied as to the defendant's guilt (see *R v Hulusi and Purvis* (1973) 58 Cr App R 378) or a witness's lack of credibility; neither must they interrupt an examination-in-chief by posing questions that appear as a cross-examination of the witness.

It is a matter of good practice that the jury pose any questions they wish to ask the witness or the trial judge in writing. The judge will pose the questions the jury wish the witnesses to answer and he or she will answer any questions the jury wish to pose to the judge in open court. Although not all questions may be considered to be appropriate, for instance in the case of *R v Pryce (Vasiliki) and Huhne (Christopher)* (2013) the trial judge thought it clear to comment on the jury's inability to understand the case before them by the very fact that they posed particular questions for example 'can a juror come to a verdict based on a reason that was not presented in court and has no facts or evidence to support it' and 'would religious conviction be a good enough reason for a wife feeling she had no choice … and he had ordered her to do something and she felt she had to obey'. The judge commented that the latter was not related to the case at all.

PREVIOUS CONSISTENT STATEMENTS OR STATEMENTS THAT SERVE THE WITNESS'S OWN PURPOSE

The discussion so far has revealed how extensive the rules of evidence are in relation to previous inconsistent statements. There is another type of statement that also requires brief consideration: previous consistent statements. It was originally permissible to prove the consistency of a witness's testimony through a previous statement made by them (see *Lutterell v Lutterell* (1670) 1 Mod 282). The general common law rule, which has now been extended and codified by the CJA 2003, prohibits this. Therefore, in both criminal and civil trials, a statement by a witness while giving testimony that they have made a consistent statement on a previous occasion is inadmissible as evidence that seeks to contribute towards the witness's creditability and the weight of their evidence – this is also known as the rule against narrative. The issue in relation to previous consistent statements relates to the risk that a witness may manufacture a statement to serve their own purpose; there is a danger that a lie could be corroborated if it was repeated to A, B and C, whose subsequent evidence is tarnished as a result. For example Mabel stands accused of assaulting Robert but intimates that she was defending herself. She tells Florian that Robert had approached her waving his fists in the air, none of which he had perceived himself – Florian had arrived while the altercation was taking place. Mabel cannot rely on the statement she made to

Florian as (a) proof of consistency in her evidence and (b) that she was defending herself. In addition, there is a risk that Florian's evidence may be spoilt as a result of the information Mabel gave him. Previous consistent statements fall outside of the traditional rule against the admission of hearsay evidence because they are being adduced to prove consistency and not as truth of the contents they contain.

KEY CASE ANALYSIS: *R v Roberts (Frederick Thomas)* **(1942) 28 Cr App R 102**

In *R v Roberts (Frederick Thomas)* (1942) 28 Cr App R 102 the defendant stood accused of murdering his ex-girlfriend. He argued in his defence that the shooting was accidental. Counsel for the defence sought to call Roberts's father to give the following evidence: the defendant had called him two days after the shooting to inform him of the 'accident'. The trial judge correctly excluded this evidence, which sought to prove that the defendant was (a) consistent in his statement and (b) the shooting really was an accident. On appeal the court held that this statement held no evidential value.

There are three exceptions to this rule in criminal cases; Figure 4.4 summarises these:

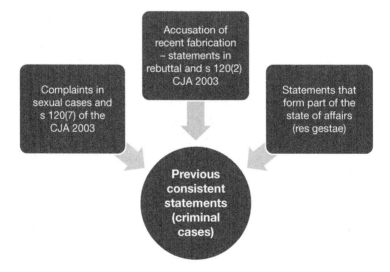

Figure 4.4 Previous consistent statements in criminal cases

COMPLAINTS IN SEXUAL CASES

The basic position is as follows: if John complains to Martha that he has been raped, then Martha can give evidence of this to prove consistency in John's allegation. The previous complaint can be oral or written (see *R v B* (1997) Crim LR 220 (CA)). Martha's evidence will assist the court in its determination of the accuracy or truthfulness of John as a witness.

KEY CASE ANALYSIS: *R v Osborne (William Henry)* (1905) 1 KB 551

Background

The defendant was accused of indecently assaulting a young girl (A). The victim was under the age of 13 and therefore the issue of consent was irrelevant. At trial evidence of a question that had been put by another child (B) to A as to why she had not waited for her to arrive at the defendant's house was admitted as evidence, A's answer to that question had expressed, to B, what the accused had done to her.

Principle established

The evidence was admitted as a previous consistent statement that lent credibility to A having been consistent in her allegation. The court laid down the following guidelines on the admission of such evidence in these cases:

- the complaint must be made by the complainant, whether male or female, contemporaneously (in relation to this point see *R v Birks* (2003) 2 Cr App R 122, CA where two months after the commission of the offence was too long a time period) and voluntarily;
- the evidence is relevant to negate consent and to prove consistency therefore it is relevant even where consent is not in issue; and
- the complainant must give evidence; the previous consistent statement cannot stand as evidence of its own accord.

The common law principle has been extended in criminal proceedings by s 120(7) of the CJA 2003, which allows such evidence to be admitted in relation to any offence provided:

- the proceedings relate to that offence;
- the conduct constitutes the offence if successfully proven;

- the witness can confirm that they made the statement; and
- that it is true to the best of their knowledge.

You should note that if, as in the scenario above, Martha chooses not to give evidence then the fact that John had made a previous statement that is consistent with his current allegation cannot assist the jury in determining consistency (or a lack of consent, see *R v White* (1999) 1 Cr App r 153). Furthermore, the complaint does not have to contain the entire elements of the offence but will normally disclose conduct that is considered unlawful. Evidence of a previous consistent statement will only be introduced by counsel where it is consistent with the witness's current testimony or as evidence to negate consent – in terms of the latter it is evidence of facts stated. You should note that counsel will only bring up the issue of consistency where the witness to whom the statement was made agrees to give evidence albeit they may be compelled to do so by witness summons in the interests of justice (see Chapter 3, s 97 of the Magistrates' Courts Act 1980 and s 2 of the Criminal Procedure (Attendance of Witnesses) Act 1965).

The trial judge will normally warn the jury that they should be careful as to the weight they attach to this evidence because it does not emanate from an independent source. The jury will decide two points: (a) was the complaint made and (b) is it consistent with the current testimony.

On-the-spot question

 What purpose is served by adducing a previous consistent statement?

The common law on the admission of previous consistent statements was preserved by s 118(1)(4) of the CJA 2003, these statements are admissible to rebut allegations of recent fabrication and as truth of facts contained therein (see also s 120(2) of the CJA 2003). Counsel may wish to adduce evidence of a previous consistent statement where the cross-examination of a witness suggests that they have recently fabricated their testimony. Such a statement will lend credit to the witness. Following on from *Nominal Defendant v Clements* (1961) 104 CLR 476 the Court of Appeal in *R v Oyesiku (Charles)* (1972) 56 Cr App R 240 confirmed that a court must consider, on an allegation of recent fabrication, the following in determining whether a previous statement is admissible as evidence of consistency:

- the level of consistency between the current testimony and the previous statement; and
- the time and circumstances in which the previous consistent statement was made; and
- whether it counters the suggestion of recent fabrication.

Statements that form part of the state of affairs (res gestae)

The term **res gestae** refers to the events, circumstances or state of affairs surrounding the commission of a criminal offence. Therefore, any statements that relate to the facts of the case are admissible as evidence of consistency and truth of facts contained therein. In *R v Fowkes* (1856) *The Times*, 8 Mar (Ch 6) 77, witness B was permitted to give evidence of the remarks 'there's the butcher' (the accused's pseudonym), which were made by witness A on seeing a face through the window. Other instances in which previous consistent statements are admissible include:

* statements that are made on accusation (see *R v Tooke (Mark Adrian)* (1990) 90 Cr App R 417);
* statements that made on the discovery of incriminating articles (also discussed in terms of inferences from silence in Chapter 6); and
* previous identifications i.e. where an identification procedure has been held under the PACE Act 1984.

In civil proceedings, s 6 of the Civil Evidence Act 1995 allows a witness, while giving evidence-in-chief, to refer to a previous consistent statement with the judge's permission. You should note that where the statement is being adduced to rebut an allegation of recent fabrication then counsel does not need to obtain the leave of the judge.

REFRESHING THE WITNESS'S MEMORY

There are instances that also require consideration: refreshing a witness's memory (a) prior to them giving evidence (out of court) and (b) while they are in the witness box giving evidence (in court).

Refreshing memory in court

The basic **rule of practice** is as follows: a witness may refer to a document made or verified by him or her to refresh their memory while in the witness box. The conditions, which apply to both civil and criminal proceedings, are set out in Figure 4.5.

The rationale behind this is to give the witness a chance to explain a mistake they may have made while giving evidence. The document may have been created by the witness or someone else, for example a police officer. In terms of the latter the witness should have read and confirmed the facts in the document. Often witnesses do not do this, for example Dirk sees something and dictates a description of it to Surinder who writes it down but does

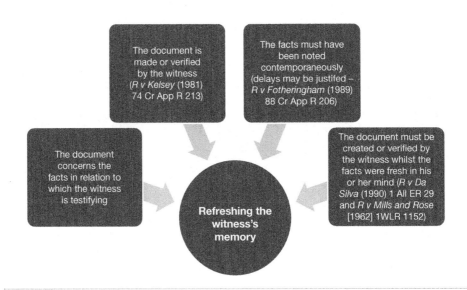

Figure 4.5 Refreshing a witness's memory

not show it to Dirk; in this situation, the rule as it stands does not permit Dirk to refresh his memory from that document. Phipson (Malek *et al*, 2012, p 268) suggests the appropriate way of dealing with this is to simply call Surinder to give evidence to confirm the description given to him by Dirk at the time. Examples of documents include a solicitor's notebook, an accurately kept logbook or the transcript of an audio-recorded conversation. The witness may only refresh his or her memory from an original document unless it has been destroyed or is unavailable, in which case the document must be proven to be accurate.

The contemporaneity by which the document is created or verified depends on the circumstances of the case and is a matter of fact; *Da Silva* highlights the application of this rule on a case-by-case basis – in this case a statement that was made over one calendar month after the event had occurred was unacceptable (see also *R v Richardson* [1971] 1 WLR 889). Whether a document meets the requirement that 'the facts be fresh in the mind of the witness when created' is a question of fact for the trial judge. It does not even matter if the witness remembers nothing until they see the statement they made; a copy of the document should also be given to the opposition. There is no statutory time limit that defines what period falls outside of these rules. However, there have been numerous cases where the court has found the time that has elapsed between the creation of a document and the event itself to be too long a delay; in *R v Graham* [1973] Crim LR 628, a four-week interval was held to be an unacceptable delay.

In criminal cases, the document used to refresh the witness's memory does not become evidence and the trial judge will warn the jury in relation to this. A document may become evidence if the opposition makes an allegation of concoction or recent fabrication in which case it will be used to help the jury determine the issue. In criminal proceedings such a document will not necessarily be exhibited for the jury to see (*R v Dillon* (1983) 85 Cr App R 29). In contrast, in civil cases the document does become an exhibit and is admissible as evidence of the facts it contains (see s 6 of the Civil Evidence Act 1995).

In addition, in criminal proceedings s 139 of the CJA 2003 provides that a person who is giving oral evidence can refresh his or her memory from a document (other than sounds and video images) that they created or verified. The section applies where an audio recording and transcript of the audio recording was made and where it is likely that the person's recollection of the events was better at that time (see also s 140 CJA 2003).

Refreshing memory out of court

Trials often take place many months after a witness might have created or verified a document. In seeking to refresh their memory, witnesses can use any means they consider appropriate even if they would not have been allowed to do so while in the witness box. Of course the witness may choose to refer to the statement they made to the police. There are obvious dangers in a witness refreshing their memory out of court, which include collusion and fabrication and there is a distinct absence of rules in relation to this.

SUMMARY

The rules (statutory and practice) on witness testimony are designed to test the evidence being put before the court while aiming for an expeditious dispensation of justice. The same rules highlight how this form of evidence must be carefully handled by both judge and jury.

FURTHER READING

Birch, D, 'A better deal for vulnerable witnesses in court' [2000] Crim LR 223.
This article explores the provisions of the Youth Justice and Criminal Evidence Act 1999 and the measures enacted to boost the chances of vulnerable witnesses being able to give best evidence.

Landa, CS (2012). *Evidence: Question and Answers 2013–2014*, 10th edn. London: Routledge.
This textbook focuses on the application of the law of evidence with some interesting practical questions and guidance on answering assessment questions.

Malek, HM, Auburn, J and Bagshaw, R (eds) (2012). *Phipson on Evidence*, 17th edn. London: Sweet & Maxwell.
This is the reference text on the law of evidence for students, academics and practitioners alike. The text is useful for detailed reference to some of the more obscure areas of evidence law.

McPeake, R (ed) (2012). *Advocacy (Bar Manuals)*, 16th edn. Oxford: Oxford University Press.
This textbook presents the skill of court advocacy and answers many of the interesting practical questions that arise as a result of the rules of evidence.

Pattenden, R, 'The Hostile Witness' (1992) 56 JCL 414.
This article explores the notion of hostile witnesses and the rationale on how they are treated as such during the course of giving evidence.

Pattenden, R, 'Canada: using a hostile witness's prior inconsistent statement for a hearsay purpose'. *International Journal of Evidence and Proof*, 2009, 13(1), 77–78.
This is an interesting note of a Canadian case; it discusses the use of a previous inconsistent statement as admissible hearsay.

Professional Standards Committee of the Bar of England and Wales, (2013), Bar Standards Board Guidance on Witness Preparation.
Available at: https://www.barstandardsboard.org.uk/code-guidance/guidance-on-witness-preparation.
This is a useful guide on the differences between witness preparation and coaching, especially in light of the decision in *R v Momodou*.

Chapter 5
The disclosure of evidence

LEARNING OUTCOMES

By the end of this chapter, you should be able to:

- Critically engage with the principles relating to the disclosure of evidence
- Understand the purpose and effect of legal professional privilege, the privilege against self-incrimination, journalistic privilege and public interest immunity on the disclosure of documents
- Determine and evaluate the rules that apply when treating evidence as being subject to privilege or immunity
- Explore the notion of disclosure and protection from disclosure, and its impact on the evidence put before the court

INTRODUCTION

The discussion in this chapter focuses on four interrelated topics relating to the disclosure of evidence, namely legal professional privilege, the privilege against self-incrimination, journalistic privilege and public interest immunity. This includes a brief look at the general rules on disclosure and their overarching purposes. We will then move on to explore the three forms of privilege and public interest immunity, all of which are vitally important to any course on evidence law.

DISCLOSURE: THE GENERAL SCHEME

Our discussion in the preceding chapters highlighted that all relevant evidence is admissible. This rule applies in equal measure to civil and criminal proceedings. In simple terms the disclosure of evidence can be stated to be the requirement to reveal something (evidence) and to do so in a timely manner – this notion will become clearer as you read through this part of the chapter.

For the purposes of criminal proceedings the Criminal Procedure and Investigations Act 1996 (CPIA) defined disclosure in criminal proceedings as set out in Figure 5.1:

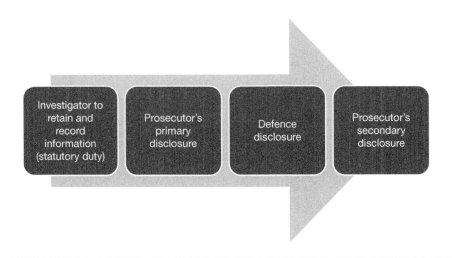

Figure 5.1 Disclosure under the old CPIA 1996 regime

You should note that the rules on disclosure are also outlined in Parts 21 and 22 of the Criminal Procedure Rules 2012 ((CrPR) as amended in April 2013). Under the old regime the prosecutor and defence were required to make disclosure prior to the trial. The rationale for this is quite simple: it allowed the parties to be prepared for trial without one side springing surprises in the form of undisclosed evidence on the other; this often led to a **cracked trial** (discontinued), which meant that the time allocated for it was wasted, witnesses were unnecessarily inconvenienced and confidence in the criminal justice system was undermined. The Secretary of State was required to issue a code of practice, which was to accompany the statute. This included a requirement for all investigators (police officers) to retain, at least until a decision on whether or not to prosecute had been made, and record material and information, for example notebooks, interview records or recordings that were collected or generated as part of the overall investigation (see s 23(1) CPIA 1996).

There was no absolute duty on the prosecutor to make a primary disclosure; it was in fact limited to any material that, in the prosecutor's opinion, might undermine the prosecution case. In response, the defence was required to disclose the nature of his or her defence but only in very general terms, for instance it should include details of any facts they wish to raise in issue and alibi etc. At this point the prosecutor's duty to make a secondary disclosure applied; the prosecution was required to disclose, wherever necessary, any material that may reasonably assist the defence (see s 3(1)(a) of the CPIA 1996).

The CJA 2003 broadened the rules on disclosure with the introduction of a single but objective test in relation to unused material held by the prosecution. As a result, s 3 of the CPIA 1996 now requires the prosecutor to disclose a copy of:

any prosecution material that has not been previously been disclosed to the accused and which might reasonably be considered capable of undermining the case for the prosecution against the accused or of assisting the case for the accused or give to the accused a written statement that there is no material of a description mentioned.

The provision defines material as something that is in the 'prosecutor's possession and which came into his or her possession in connection with the case for the prosecution against the accused which . . . he has inspected in connection with the case for the prosecution against the accused'. The copy can be a scanned version of the document, therefore change in its form is also permitted. Where the prosecutor deems giving a copy of it undesirable or impracticable then he or she should make provision for the accused to inspect it instead. Section 3(6) strictly prohibits the disclosure of any material that the court orders as being not in the public interest to disclose (see also s 17 of the Regulation of Investigatory Powers Act 2000, which restricts the disclosure of material obtained from, among other things, the interception of communications and surveillance). Figure 5.2 (below) represents the current position on disclosure.

Section 6A(1), inserted into the CPIA 1996 by the Criminal Justice and Immigration Act 2008 (CJIA) and the CJA 2003, provides that the defence should disclose:

a written statement setting out the nature of the accused's defence, including any particular defences on which he intends to rely. [This should indicate] the matters of fact on which he takes issue with the prosecution [and set out in relation to each matter] why he [or she] takes issue with the prosecution. [They

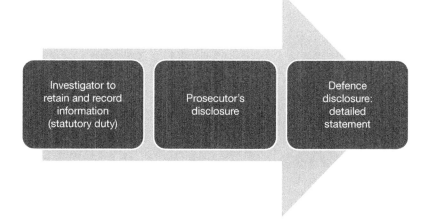

Figure 5.2 Disclosure under the CJA 2003 (new regime)

should also indicate] any point of law (including any point as to the admissibility of evidence or an abuse of process) which he wishes to take, and any authority on which he intends to rely for that purpose.

Furthermore, where the statement discloses an alibi the defence must give details in relation to this that includes:

the name, address and date of birth of any witness the accused believes is able to give evidence in support of the alibi, or as many of those details as are known to the accused when the statement is given [and] any information in the accused's possession which might be of material assistance in identifying or finding any such witness [whose details are not known to the accused at the time he or she makes the statement].

Alibi evidence will tend to support the contention that the accused was elsewhere at the time the offence was committed.

In civil cases the rules on disclosure are set out in Part 31 of the Civil Procedure Rules 2013 (CPR). The extent of the disclosure that is required is dictated by the track upon which the case is registered to proceed. Simply put, a track is a set course or path for a claim. Therefore, the rationale for having three tracks – small, fast and multi-track – is based partly around the amount of work that has to be done in relation to certain types of case by reason of its value and complexity. For example a complex breach of contract that is valued over £100,000 with more than four parties involved, each of whom claims against the other, would normally be listed on the multi-track. In contrast, suing your neighbour in a money dispute (£100) would be suitable for the small claims track. Track allocation occurs after the parties have filed (submitted to the court) their 'allocation questionnaires' – these are documents that gather information so that the court can allocate the case to the most suitable track. Track allocation will take place after the parties have already filed the particulars of claim (claim form), defence, counterclaim or counter-defence. Figure 5.3 (below) outlines the criteria for allocation to each track.

The rules set down in Part 31 of the CPR apply to all civil cases other than those on the small claims track (CPR 31.1(2)). The rules refer to the disclosure and inspection of documents; these are (a) anything in which information of any description is recorded and (b) a copy of the same, which means anything onto which information recorded in the document has been copied, by whatever means and whether directly or indirectly. The requirements laid down in CPR Rule 35.1 are to give standard disclosure. You should note that the court may, of its own volition, dispense with or even limit standard disclosure, the parties may do this too but it must be done in writing.

CPR Rule 31.6 defines standard disclosure as requiring a party to disclose:

Small
- All cases: value less than £5000, or
- In personal injury cases the damages for pain, suffering and loss of amenity must be less than £1000, otherwise they go to the fast track
- On conclusion the costs of litigation are recovered by the winner from the loser

Fast
- Value between £5000–£15,000
- On conclusion only fixed costs are recovered by the winner from the loser

Multi
- All other case are listed here and any valued at below £5000, but that contain complex or technical issues

Figure 5.3 Track allocation under the Civil Procedure Rules 2013

- any documents on which they will be relying;
- any documents that (a) adversely affect his or her own case, (b) adversely affect any other party's claim, (c) support any other party's claim and (d) they are require to disclose by a relevant **Practice Direction**.

The CPR was last updated in July 2013; there are regular updates on the website that you can access here: www.justice.gov.uk/courts/procedure-rules/civil.

On-the-spot questions

Why do you think disclosure is required for the efficient administration of justice?

Explore the rules on disclosure under the CrPR and the CPR. What, if any, are the differences?

PRIVILEGE AND PUBLIC INTEREST IMMUNITY

Any discussion on disclosure also requires consideration of the related doctrines that protect information from being disclosed. In this part of the chapter the discussion will focus on the doctrines of privilege and public interest immunity. Figure 5.4 summarises the two doctrines:

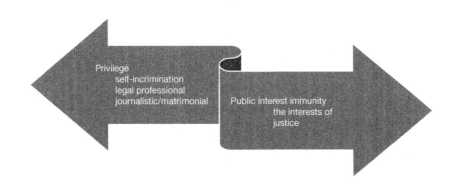

Figure 5.4 Privilege and public interest immunity

Privilege(s)

The current law requires certain classifications of evidence to be revealed and to be done so in a timely and unobstructed manner so as to promote the **administration of justice**. There are, however, specified instances in which English law regards certain information as needing protection from being forcibly disclosed. Privilege is not a right but an exemption that is claimed by the party seeking to protect particular information from forced disclosure and it will only belong to them. Where a claim fails then evidence must be disclosed. Where a question is posed in an assessment ask yourself the following questions in this order: (a) is the evidence relevant and admissible? and (b) is it subject to privilege or immunity from disclosure? The answers must be (a) yes and (b) no, if the evidence is to be disclosed. The forms of privilege that will be discussed in this part of the chapter are:

- privilege against self-incrimination
- legal and professional or litigation privilege
- negotiations that are without prejudice
- journalistic privilege.

These are the common categories that will normally appear in most good courses on evidence law. The distinction between privilege and public interest immunity lies in the fact that the *former attaches itself to the evidence that is justified because of its connection to an individual and the latter seeks to protect information from disclosure because that may result in a threat to national security* (discussed on p 68).

Privilege against self-incrimination

The doctrine of privilege was developed in the common law; this particular form of privilege provides that a witness in court proceedings is not required to (a) answer any question put to them nor (b) produce a document, where that would (c) incriminate themselves and therefore potentially (d) expose them to a charge for the commission of an offence contrary to the criminal law or (e) **forfeiture** in England, Scotland and Wales. The Latin maxim that is literally translated as 'nobody can be forced to give him or herself away' (*nemo tenetur prodere se ipsum*) sums up this privilege (see *Blunt v Park Lane Hotel Ltd* [1942] 2 KB 253). You should note the following: if Josh gives any answers that incriminate him then those answers will only be evidence against him and not anyone else. A refusal to answer questions in cross-examination must not relate to any criminal offence with which they stand charged or questions that seek to establish their guilt (see s 101 of the CJA 2003 on an accused's bad character and s 1(2) of the Criminal Evidence Act (CEA) 1898).

No rule of law exists requiring a judge to warn a witness that they do not have to answer incriminating questions. Questioning during cross-examination can be direct or indirect, therefore this stage of the trial process must be approached with care because accidental responses, documents produced or responses made by a witness in ignorance of their right cannot be later retracted. In terms of the latter two, the court may rely on the evidence and the witness will not be eligible to appeal on the ground that the document or information was privileged. However, the situation is more complex when an accidental response leads to the discovery of evidence – in this case it is submitted that the subsequently discovered evidence should remain admissible but the response should not (see *Rank Film Distributors v Video Information Centre* [1982] AC 380 and *Tate Access Floors Inc v Boswell* [1990] 3 All ER 303). It follows that if Magda, through cross-examination, is forced into answering a question on something in terms of which she has successfully claimed privilege then any answer that she gives is inadmissible for the purposes of bringing subsequent proceedings against her. In *R v Garbett* (1847) 1 Den CC 236 the court held that these answers were comparable to involuntary confessions and therefore should be inadmissible.

It makes sense therefore that on a successful claim of privilege an accused can refuse to answer any question related to a criminal offence with which they do not stand charged, unless of course privilege is itself **statute barred**. You should note that if Dorothy chooses to answer such a question then that would amount to her confessing to the commission of an offence contrary to English or European Union criminal law (see also the Communities Act 1972). Where the offence would be contrary to the law of another jurisdiction then the authorities, in some circumstances, may have a duty to disclose the offence for which there is a discreet process (internet search terms: international police). However, s 14(1) of the Civil Evidence Act 1969 provides that in civil proceedings this privilege does not cover the witness being exposed to criminal or civil proceedings outside of the UK (or EU). Therefore, Kate cannot claim privilege on the basis that she may be subjected to criminal charges or civil proceedings in Norway.

The importance of an accused's right not to incriminate him or herself is also recognised under the right to a fair trial provided by Article 6 of the ECHR (see *Saunders v United Kingdom* (1997) A/702 23 EHRR 313). In the broader scheme of things, this privilege is related to an accused's right to remain silent, a right that in modern day English law has been somewhat eroded by the Criminal Justice and Public Order Act 1994 (as discussed in Chapter 6).

A successful claim for this privilege will mean that a witness may not be cross-examined in such a way as to obtain the evidence that is protected. This does not preclude the party opposing the claim to prove the same thing using other evidence or an alternative method, for example Elizabeth may have successfully claimed privilege against self-incrimination preventing a document from being revealed however Harry may then adduce William as a witness against Elizabeth to give evidence that may prove the same thing.

KEY CASE ANALYSIS: *Rio Tinto Zinc Corporation and Others v Westinghouse Electric Corporation* **[1978] AC 547**

Background

This case concerned an alleged breach of contract for the construction of nuclear power stations. Westinghouse was a Virginian (USA) company and it claimed that the contract was frustrated by reason of a uranium shortage caused by its producers fixing its price in an unlawful cartel, this included two English companies of which Rio Tinto was one. A Virginian judge made two requests to the High Court (London): the first was to ask it to order a number of senior officials connected to the companies to appear in the Consular Offices of the USA in London so that they could be cross-examined. The second request was to require Rio Tinto to disclose particular documents. The orders were duly made. However the company made a claim for privilege on the basis that it could not disclose some of the documents because they would incriminate it under the Treaty of the European Economic Community (now subsumed into the European Union). The effect of disclosure would have been to expose Rio Tinto to heavy fines for anti-competitive practices because the treaty had been directly incorporated into English law.

Principle established

Both the High Court (London) and the Virginian court upheld the claim, the latter on the basis of the Fifth Amendment (USA Constitution). Shortly after this the US department for justice initiated a grand jury investigation for breaches of US anti-trust law and requested the witnesses be compelled to give evidence. Section 6002/2 of the US Constitution provided that evidence obtained where privilege against self-incrimination is claimed in respect of one set of proceedings cannot be used in subsequent criminal proceedings in other matters. Thus, if Rio Tinto were to give evidence then that evidence could not be used in the breach of contract claim. This matter reached the English Court of Appeal that decided the claim for privilege be upheld because of the unlawful manner in which the grand jury investigation had been extended internationally. This would be an infringement of the UK's sovereignty and her Majesty's courts could take this into account when declaring her government's policy.

The trial judge must assess all the circumstances of the case before deciding whether there is a 'real and appreciable danger' of the witness, if they answer the question that is being put to them, exposing themselves to criminal or civil proceedings (see *R v Boyes* (1861) 30 LJQB 301). Where the prosecution promises not to proceed with a prosecution then privilege will not be granted (see *A&T Istel v Tully* [1993] AC 45). However, you should note that if the prosecution reneges on its promise then the witness may have a potential case for an **abuse of the court's process**. The privilege against self-incrimination does not have retrospective application therefore the claim must be made prior to the provision of information or any charge, for example if Simon has given information that incriminates him or he has already been charged with the commission of a criminal offence, for instance fraud, then he cannot subsequently claim privilege.

The privilege is an integral part of an individual's right to a fair trial under Article 6 of the ECHR. The jurisprudence of the European Court of Human Rights (ECtHR) has confirmed this fact; see also *Saunders v UK* (1997) 18 EHRR CD 23.

Exceptions (statutory)

Figure 5.5 summarises the statutory exceptions to the privilege against self-incrimination:

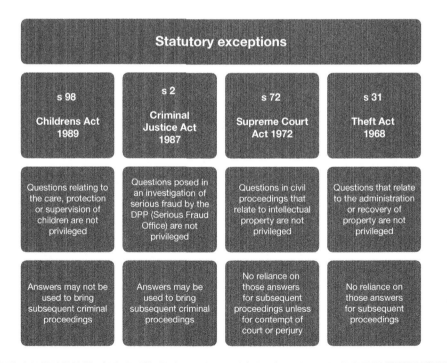

Figure 5.5 Exceptions to the privilege against self-incrimination

On-the-spot questions

Summarise the rationale that underpins the privilege against self-incrimination in English law.

What requirements, if any, must be satisfied to claim the privilege against self-incrimination and what is the extent of the protection provided?

In what instance can a court use answers given by a witness relating to privileged information as evidence?

Legal or professional and litigation privilege

In stark contrast to the privilege against self-incrimination this form of privilege focuses on the following:

- Legal or professional privilege protects confidential communication and evidence of that provided it takes place in the course of normal legal practice between a client and their lawyer.
- Litigation privilege protects confidential communication and evidence of that between a lawyer and/or their client with a third party provided it is created with the dominant purpose of obtaining legal advice in contemplation of litigation.

The privilege affects the 'confidential communication', which is defined as a document that conveys information. This could be audio or visual and includes emails, letters and photographs, and also draft letters or instructions that may have never been sent provided the criteria (discussed shortly) is established (see *Southwark and Vauxhall Water Co v Quick* (1878) 3 QBD 315). This form of privilege attaches itself to the original document and the proof of its contents can be established through the oral evidence of a witness, regardless of how they came by it (see *Calcraft v Guest* [1889] 1 QB 759). You will see that documents such as MOTs, accident reports and service records cannot be privileged because they will not satisfy the requirements. Although you should note that these may be tendered as evidence to prove other things i.e. the fitness of a car on the road in a claim of negligence.

In terms of legal or professional privilege this would include instances in which someone obtains legal advice from a lawyer and where a lawyer gives that advice, this does not cover communications between the lawyer and/or their client with a third party. Litigation privilege covers communications between the lawyer and/or their client with a third party and may relate to instances in which information is sought prior to a claim being made, for example a report by an expert that confirms that a particular course of action was professionally negligent.

These two forms of privilege can only be claimed by the party to whom the communication belongs regardless of whenever the litigation may occur. A successful claim will mean that confidential communications are immune from being disclosed. In *R v Derby Magistrates' court, ex parte B* [1996] 3 WLR 681 the court held that individuals should be able to display candour and consult their lawyers with the confidence that their discussion will never have been revealed without their consent. The court was of the opinion that the administration of justice rests upon this fundamental rule of evidence. You should note that there have been some inroads into this form of privilege with the Proceeds of Crime Act 2002 and in terms of child protection and safety.

Legal or professional privilege protects communications between a lawyer and his or her client provided it is created in the usual course of legal practice. This form of privilege cannot protect communications where the relationship of lawyer and client does not exist. The client may decide that he or she wants the communication to be disclosed, perhaps because they are not concerned about its disclosure. Where Surinder writes to Mark, a solicitor friend of his, asking for legal advice on the purchase of a vintage car, then the communication will be privileged because the advice obtained is legal advice even though Surinder subsequently chooses to appoint Jay, a barrister, to conduct the transaction (see *Minter v Priest* [1930] AC 558). Communications between a lawyer and client that are not for obtaining legal advice will not attract privilege. Communications will only be privileged if the following two conditions are satisfied:

- the nature of the communication must be confidential; and
- the communication must be made in the course of a lawyer and client relationship or with the prospect of establishing such a relationship.

The party who claims privilege has the duty to ensure that it continues; this will be automatic unless the opposition can prove that the client or the lawyer created the communication itself in the furtherance of a criminal offence or fraud (see *R v Central Criminal Court, ex parte Francis and Francis* [1989] AC 346), or that the holder of the privilege has chosen to waive it, which they are entitled to do. You should note that, as discussed earlier, an accidental, ignorant or wilful disclosure of information that is protected by privilege being admissible as evidence. Furthermore, privilege does not end where the relationship between the lawyer and his or her client terminates (see *R v Barton* [1973] 1 WLR 115 and *R v Ataou* [1988] 2 All ER 321).

If the opposition obtains privileged information through some means of deception then the holder of the privilege can obtain an injunction preventing the opposition from utilising it. An injunction will not be ordered where privilege was either waived or lost however the use of the communication as evidence, even though it is most likely to have already satisfied the requirements on relevance, will still have to adhere to the standard rules relating to admissibility (see *R v Tompkins* (1977) 67 Cr App R 181).

A lawyer who is jointly acting for both a claimant and defendant should take care in ensuring that relevant communication is protected by privilege (see *Buttes Gas & Oil Co v Hammer (No. 3)* [1981] 1 QB 223). Clients always have the option of claiming that his or her lawyer has acted in a manner that is professionally negligent where the lawyer accidently discloses a privileged communication. Legal or professional privilege acts to protect property from seizure (see s 8 and s 10 the PACE Act 1984) unless the communication is in furtherance of a criminal offence or a fraud.

It is important to realise the extent to which legal professional privilege can be waived. Jonathan holds privilege for documents X, Y and Z. Each of the documents cross-refers to the other. His agreement to waive privilege in document X does not affect his privilege in the other documents. References to documents Y and Z will be blacked out in document X.

Communications between a lawyer and his or her client with a third party will only be privileged if the following criteria, set out in *Three Rivers District Council v Governor and Company of the Bank of England* [2004] UKHL 48, are satisfied:

- there must be a genuine prospect of litigation occurring;
- the purpose or dominant purpose (where there is more than one) of the communication must be to obtain legal advice for pending or contemplated litigation; and
- the communication must be made within a relevant legal context.

Where litigation is neither contemplated nor pending, a claim for privilege cannot be made (see *Wheeler v Le Marchant* (1881) 17 Ch D 675). Lord Wilberforce highlighted in *Waugh v British Railways Board* [1980] AC 521 that privilege helps induce candour, which is not required if the purpose of obtaining advice is something else. His comments demonstrate the fact that there is a fine balance to be achieved between the administration and interests of justice through the disclosure of relevant and admissible evidence that proves causation, namely that X caused Y, and the promotion of candour between a lawyer and his or her client so that a case may be fully prepared. To achieve this, the application of legal or professional privilege should be limited to communications that are created with the purpose or dominant purpose of obtaining legal advice for pending or contemplated litigation. Therefore, where more than one purpose exists then the dominant purpose must be obtaining legal advice for pending or contemplated litigation. The decision confirms that limiting legal or professional privilege to those instances in which the only purpose was pending or contemplated litigation or to extend it to those where the purposes were equal would undermine the rationale that underpins this form of privilege. For instance, following a spate of small workplace accidents Mehta Factories Ltd seek advice from Barristers Inc on the compliance of their policies with current health and safety law, and how they may minimise the risk of a potential claim being made against them. There are two clear equal purposes here: regulatory compliance and the reduction of risk after the spate of small workplace accidents – this communication would clearly not be privileged (see also *Grant v Downs*, 135 CLR 674).

KEY CASE ANALYSIS: *Three Rivers District Council v Governor and Company of the Bank of England (No 5)* **[2005] EWCA Civ 933**

Background

After the collapse of the BCCI Bank, a party of claimants (creditors and liquidators) made a claim against the Bank of England (BoE) for malfeasance in public office (a failure on the part of the BoE to adequately supervise BCCI's activities). The claimants sought disclosure of communications relating to an inquiry that the BCCI's lawyers had made with the BBCI. The BCCI claimed privilege.

Principle established

The trial judge held that the communications were not privileged because they were not created with the purpose of either obtaining or seeking legal advice relating to the BCCI's legal obligations and rights. The judge commented that the BBCI, in claiming privilege, was seeking to attract the least possible criticism.

The case highlights that a relevant legal context includes advice that is given for the purpose of enhancing the prospects of successfully claiming or defending an action

---

On-the-spot question

 What was the significance of the decision in *Waugh v British Railways Board* [1980] AC 521?

Without prejudice negotiations

Generally, oral or written communications that are termed 'without prejudice' cannot be used as evidence of guilt. However, simply labelling an email or a letter as being 'without prejudice' does not automatically provide it with immunity from being disclosed as evidence; it is the intention of the parties in creating it that does. Such communication will promote candour (see *Cutts v Head* [1984] Ch 290) and the overriding objectives of expediency and progression as set out in the Civil and Criminal Procedure rules respectively and the notions of alternative dispute resolution (see also CPR Part 36).

KEY CASE ANALYSIS: *Rush and Tompkins v Greater London Council* **[1989] AC 1280**

In this case without prejudice negotiations had taken place between X and Y which had led to a settlement. These negotiations were privileged and therefore could not be disclosed to Z. X had entered into a building contract with Y who had subcontracted Z. X sued Y and Z but through without prejudice negotiations had settled with Y. Z applied to the court for discovery and disclosure of these but Y claimed they were privileged. The court at first instance agreed, the Court of Appeal disagreed and ordered discovery. Y appealed to the House of Lords who decided that the without prejudice rule made any subsequent litigation that was connected with the same proof of any admissions made with the intention of reaching a settlement inadmissible. Admissions that were made to settle with a different party in the same litigation were generally inadmissible regardless of whether settlement was actually achieved. Public policy applied to protect such negotiations from being disclosed to a third party too.

The Court of Appeal confirmed the following in terms of without prejudice communications:

- They promote negotiation and early settlement without risk of accruing liability.
- Using appropriate terminology (express limitation) means that particular parts of the communication, although privileged, can be referred where there is no settlement, for example for the apportionment of costs.
- Privilege of the communication is not dependent on the existence of proceedings.
- The court may look at a communication marked as being without prejudice for the purpose of deciphering the terms of a settlement.
- This privilege extends to the communications of the lawyers and their clients.

In terms of the second point, this is known as a Calderbank limitation (from *Calderbank v Calderbank* [1976] Fam 93). In this case A (wife) and B (husband) were married. A had inherited a sum over £80,000 and was appealing against an order that required her to pay a sum of £10,000 in costs for ancillary relief proceedings; essentially each was ordered to pay their own. A sought to adduce a without prejudice letter that her solicitors had sent to B's solicitors, which contained details of the fact that she had offered to pay far in excess of the £10,000 ordered. She also relied on an affidavit in which she proposed to transfer property worth £12,000 to B. The court decided that the offer she had made could be disclosed to the court after the final order was made in proceedings for ancillary relief and thereby could achieve costs benefits that would accrue if a payment into court had been made.

The effect of this is as follows: John offers to settle with Jan subject to a without prejudice communication that contains the following express limitation: if costs, after the claim is adjudicated upon, proved excessive or unnecessary then John can refer to the offer to settle and request that the court reduce the costs apportioned to him because Jan could have settled the matter earlier and avoided the excessive or unnecessary costs incurred. This form of privilege still continues to apply after the matter has been settled.

Journalistic privilege

This form of privilege protects the source of information from being disclosed (see *British Steel v Granada Corporation* [1981] AC 1096). Section 10 of the Contempt of Court Act 1981 provides the statutory basis for journalistic privilege by stating that:

> . . . [a] court may [not] require a person to disclose, nor [find] any person guilty of contempt of court for refusing to disclose, the source of information [that is] contained in a publication for which [they are] responsible, unless . . . disclosure is necessary in the interests of justice or national security or for the prevention of disorder or crime.

The provision is construed widely to cover direct and indirect reference (see *Maxwell v Pressdram* [1987] 1 WLR 298).

Public interest immunity

The fair and efficient administration of justice lies at the heart of an adversarial justice system that requires relevant and admissible evidence to be brought before a court so that a matter may be adjudicated upon; such a system operates in the United Kingdom. The notion of the **public interest** concerns an idea in political philosophy that relates to the transformation of the interests of 'the public' into a notion of 'common good or interest'. Giving effect to common good is also considered to be the general purpose of government and law.

Claims for immunity are most often made by those in public office and relate to affairs of the state for instance they are made by government ministers or members of parliament however private individuals can also claim immunity as demonstrated by *D v NSPCC* [1978] AC 171. The basis of the claims will lie in one of the following reasons:

* government policy documents;
* local or national documents concerning national security or high-level state affairs;
* confidential documents;
* documents that relate to crime (detection or prevention).

Government policy documents often contain politically sensitive content and therefore will be eligible for protection. Documents containing the identity of informants or whistle-blowers or details of surveillance posts (see *R v Johnson* [1968] 1 All ER 121) will be protected so as to continue to promote the detection and prevention of crime. In terms of the latter, immunity will be dependent upon whether the document proves the innocence of the accused (discussed later).

Ministers often sought immunity on the basis that the nature of the document required it – perhaps it contains sensitive information (a contents claim: see *Air Canada v Secretary of State for Trade (No 2)* [1983] 2 AC 394). Immunity was also sought on the ground that the document fell into a class of documents that should be protected (a class claim).

Immunity seeks protection of documents because disclosure of them would present a threat to national security, be prejudicial to the general public good and perhaps even undermine individual freedoms. Confidentiality by its nature requires the limitation of the information that is disclosed. The rationale that underpins this doctrine rests upon the argument that justice for a private individual is outweighed by the interest of the public in protecting certain types of communication from disclosure. However, you should note that where a document would prove an individual's innocence then the balance would favour the individual and avoidance of a miscarriage of justice (see *R v Keane* [1994] 1 WLR 746). Figure 5.6 summarises the reasoning from *Rogers v Home Secretary* [1973] AC 388 and those factors that the court will consider after having considered the necessity of disclosure (in both civil and criminal proceedings) when determining (balancing) whether immunity should or should not be granted:

In criminal cases immunity on the basis of public interest is governed by ss 21(1) and (2) of the CPIA 1996. The provisions state that:

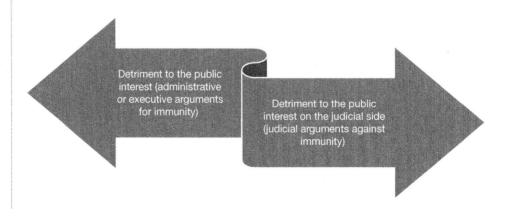

Figure 5.6 Balancing the detriment

> . . . where this Part applies [with regard to] things failing to be done after the
> relevant time in [terms of] an alleged offence . . . [the common law rules that]
> . . . were effective immediately before the appointed day [that] relate to the
> disclosure of [prosecution] material . . . do not apply . . . [this] does not affect the
> [common law rules] on disclosure in the public interest.

Historically, claims for public interest immunity were criticised as being almost
predetermined when in fact they were open to be challenged. This led them to further
scrutiny. Although the confidential working of government is required for operational
reasons (effective working without impediment) there will be occasions when the public
interest requires this to be disclosed.

In *Conway v Rimmer* [1968] AC 910 the House of Lords was presented with a claim for
public interest immunity, in civil actions, concerning documents held by the police and
certificates declaring immunity issued by a government minister. The house decided that,
regardless of the minister's certificate, the court was still entitled to consider the issue of
whether a communication was immune from disclosure on the basis of the public interest.
The court would take into account the minister's views. The argument that the court was
not able to assess the nature of the communications and the repercussions was rejected; it
was not reasonable to allow ministers to exclude whole classes of documents without that
decision being scrutinised. In the present case the house decided that it would give great
weight to protecting the confidentiality of the Inland Revenue's documents relating to tax.
You should note however that the court would usually avoid scrutinising documents that
are considered to be high-level and related to national security.

In *Burmah Oil v Bank of England* [1980] AC 1090 the House of Lords confirmed that there
would be instances in which confidentiality of documents must be preserved, for instance
cabinet papers from matters discussing national security. It also stated that the initial grant
of immunity would only be made on strong grounds and this also means that any
counterclaims would have to be equally strong.

There are a number of conflicting decisions on whether immunity can be waived once it is
granted. *Rogers v Home Secretary* [1973] AC 388 suggests that it cannot, however in
Campbell v Tameside MBC [1982] QB 1065 the court decided that waiver depended on the
level of the document, for instance if it was a low-level policy document then waiver would
be permitted provided the author agreed. The court would consider the significance of the
document and whether it would be in the public interest not to disclose it. The ECtHR has
recognised the need to protect certain documents from disclosure (see *Rowe v UK* (2000)
30 EHRR 1), for instance for the preservation of national security while safeguarding
adversarial justice and the right to a fair trial.

The judge, a party to the proceedings or a government minister may raise an objection to
the disclosure of a document, the court would then decide the issue of immunity at a
separate hearing (civil proceedings) or within a **voir dire** (criminal proceedings).

On-the-spot questions

What is the rationale that underpins a claim for public interest immunity?

What factors does the court take into account when considering whether to grant immunity?

SUMMARY

Disclosure in criminal proceedings is governed by the CPIA 1996 and in civil proceedings under the Civil Procedure Rules 2012 (Part 31). Privilege seeks to protect evidence from disclosure on the following grounds: legal or professional, litigation, self-incrimination, without prejudice negotiations and journalistic. A successful claim for public interest immunity permits documents to be withheld on the basis that it would be contrary (prejudicial) to the public interest.

FURTHER READING

Birdling, M, 'Self-incrimination goes to Strasbourg: *O'Halloran and Francis v United Kingdom.*'
   International Journal of Evidence and Proof, 2008, 12(1), 58–63.
This article discusses the ECtHR's reconsideration of the privilege against self-incrimination as an implied right under Article 6 of the ECtHR. The decision is important as it reconciles the apparent disparity between the approach of the UK courts and ECtHR.

Kirk, D, 'How do you solve a problem like disclosure?' (2013) 77(4) JCL 275.
This article explores the Attorney General's proposed guidelines on disclosure and the draft Judicial Protocol on the disclosure of unused material in criminal cases.

Landa, CS (2012). *Evidence: Question and Answers 2013–2014*, 10th edn. London: Routledge.
This textbook focuses on the application of the law of evidence with some interesting practical questions and guidance on answering assessment questions.

Parkinson, S, 'Fairness and public interest immunity: inconsistent concepts?' (2004) 154(7111)
   NLJ 46.
This article focuses on the authorities for balancing the considerations for a public interest immunity claim using a fictional case and judge.

Chapter 6
Silence, identification, lies and warnings

LEARNING OUTCOMES

By the end of this chapter, you should be able to:

- Critically engage with the legal principles relating to the right to silence
- Determine the effect of silence on accusation
- Identify the circumstances in which the court may draw adverse inferences
- Understand how the court treats lies and the use of care warnings
- Highlight the importance of Turnbull Warnings and Lucas Directions

INTRODUCTION

In this chapter the discussion will focus on the rules relating to the silence of a defendant when they are accused of having committed a criminal offence. This will include a brief look at how the right to silence has been eroded by contemporary legislation. Then the chapter will move on to consider care warnings and lies, identification evidence and directions to the jury on the use of evidence that may be regarded as suspicious.

SILENCE

Fairness has dictated the English law's long-standing tradition of preserving an accused's right to remain silent and as discussed affording them the privilege against self-incrimination. The current law provides a qualified right to silence; prior to this an accused could remain silent during a police interview nor were they required to give evidence in their own defence and the court could not take this as evidence of their guilt (see Chapter 5).

People are often found in situations that may seem incriminating, for instance Donley sees a blood-soaked Jack standing over Paul's body. On being questioned by Donley, Jack says nothing because he wishes to protect the identity of the assailant. Most people, at some point in their lives, will have been asked a question to which they have responded immediately; similarly the common perception is that innocent people respond to an accusation immediately because they have nothing to hide, but the law also accepts that individuals may remain silent for a variety of reasons, even though the motive for doing so is only relevant to the mitigation of a sentence.

The Criminal Justice and Public Order Act 1994 (CJPOA) has eroded the right to silence by allowing a jury to draw **adverse inferences** from the silence of an accused where they are under investigation (including questioning under caution) or being tried for a criminal offence – the proposals that this Act adopted were opposed by the Royal Commission on Criminal Justice when asked to report on them.

Common law

The 1994 Act did not affect the common law rules that existed in relation to silence, in general terms the silence of an accused is irrelevant. The common law provides that an accused has the right to remain silent. Where parties are on equal speaking terms then it is reasonable to expect a response from the accused, regardless of whether that is an acceptance or denial; this is one occasion when the accused's silence under the common law may suggest that they accept the allegation or charge (*R v Mitchell* (1982) 17 Cox CC 503). The trial judge will have to answer two questions of law to determine this: (a) were the parties on an equal footing and (b) could an unequivocal response be reasonably expected in the circumstances at the time. You should note that a conversation between John and a police officer would not fall under this.

On-the-spot question

 Summarise the extent of the right to silence under the common law.

CJPOA 1994

Sections 34–37 regulate particular occasions on which the silence of an accused may lead to the jury drawing adverse inferences against them. The aim of the scheme was to reduce the reliance on silence as a tool to evade justice and to promote early admission or denial so that the criminal justice process was not delayed. Therefore, Tunde can choose to remain silent on an accusation but he may open himself up to possible adverse inferences being drawn against him. The scheme will apply to Tunde if he:

- fails or refuses to mention facts on being questioned in an authorised place of detention, facts that he later seeks to rely on in his defence (s 34);
- fails or refuses to testify at court (s 35);
- fails or refuses to account for, in an authorised place of detention, incriminating objects, marks or substances (s 36); or
- fails or refuses to account for, in an authorised place of detention, his presence in an incriminating place.

You should note that the Youth Justice and Criminal Evidence Act 1999 amended the CJPOA and that any evidence that falls under ss 34, 36 and 37 is still subject to the normal rules on admission and therefore exclusion, regardless of the possible adverse inferences that may be drawn from it. For example, if Tunde is unlawfully searched and that results in an incriminating object being recovered from him then that evidence may be excluded under the PACE Act 1984 because of the manner in which it was obtained.

Section 34

The aim of this provision is to promote the early disclosure of any defence or material fact that may support the same. This provision has caused the courts difficulties in terms of interpretation but covers questioning:

- *before being charged* with the commission of a criminal offence but while under caution;
- *on being charged* with the commission of a criminal offence or being officially informed that there is a possibility of them being prosecuted for the same.

The condition prior to the jury being able to draw an adverse inference is that the individual should be given access to legal advice (inserted into the 1994 Act as s 34(2A) of the YJCEA 1999). The accused must fail or refuse to mention a fact when questioned under caution before charge and under investigation that they later look to rely on in his or her defence.

The effect of the provision only applies once the individual has been cautioned, this is because it is the first opportunity the individual is made aware that they are opening themselves up to potential adverse inferences being drawn if they remain silent and then subsequently try to rely on a fact. The questioning must take place in an authorised place of detention; this is most often a police station but also includes designated areas in airports and shipping ports. For example Julia is questioned under caution at Marylebone Police Station by PC Frances; she fails to mention that she punched Marcus because she felt a threat of unlawful personal violence towards her (self-defence). Julia later seeks to rely on this fact as a defence at trial; it is possible that an adverse inference will be drawn against her initial failure.

KEY CASE ANALYSIS: *R v Argent* [1997] 2 Cr App R 27

Background

The accused appealed against conviction and sentence for manslaughter. After receiving legal advice he refused to answer subsequent questions. The trial judge refused to admit the first police interview but admitted the second because it was accompanied by a positive identification. He also directed the jury that they could draw adverse inferences from his silence.

Principle established

The court reject the appeal however Lord Bingham set out the conditions that must be satisfied before an adverse inference is drawn, these are:

- proceedings for the commission of a criminal offence must exist;
- the failure to mention the fact must be before or on charge;
- the failure must have occurred while the accused was being questioned under caution;
- the questioning must seek to establish the person who committed the offence;
- the fact must be relied upon in defence;
- it must have been reasonable to expect the accused to mention that fact when questioned taking into account the circumstances at the time.

The legal test is twofold: (a) what could the accused be reasonably expected to mention (objective) and (b) what could they have mentioned (subjective). The court will take into account a number of factors when considering these questions, including their age, intoxication, mental and physical state and any legal advice they received. Note: this list is not exhaustive.

Facts may be raised by the accused him- or herself or a witness giving evidence, whether in examination-in-chief or cross-examination. The latter includes prosecution witnesses, for example if Kwame's barrister cross-examines a prosecution witness and thereby puts a fact (not mere speculative theory) in defence to them, then the accused will be open to an adverse inference being drawn against him provided the conditions are satisfied namely it must be relied upon (*R v N* [1998] 1 WLR 153; *R v Weber* [2004] 1 Crim App R 40).

Once the criteria have been established, the jury can draw such inferences that they consider to be properly drawn from the evidence. An adverse inference will undermine the case of the accused but is not in itself enough to sustain a conviction. The trial judge will direct the jury and remind them of any excuse the accused gave when failing to mention the fact that he or she subsequently relied on.

Section 35

If an accused fails to testify in court then the jury may draw an adverse inference. The provision states:

> . . . the court shall, at the conclusion of the evidence for the prosecution, satisfy itself . . . that the accused is aware that the stage has been reached at which evidence can be given for the defence and that he can . . . give evidence and that, if he chooses not to . . . or having been sworn, without good cause refuses to answer any question, it will be permissible for the court or jury to draw such inferences as appear proper.

There is no requirement on the accused to give evidence, therefore issues of contempt and compellability do not arise. The trial judge should make sure that the accused is aware of repercussions of not testifying (Under Practice Direction (Crown Court: Evidence: Advice to a Defendant) [1995] 2 Cr App R 192). This provision will only apply once the prosecution has established its case (see *R v Cowan* [1996] QB 373).

In *R v Kavanagh* [2005] EWHC 820 (Admin) the accused failed to give evidence because he was suffering from depression; the magistrates did not draw an adverse inference because of this. The court is not under an obligation to draw the inference but it must consider, on the basis of the evidence available to it, the reasons why the accused did not do so.

The trial judge should also remind the jury that silence on its own it not enough to form the basis of a conviction. The basic inference the jury can draw is that the accused has no answer to the allegation.

Section 36

This provision states that:

> . . . where a person is arrested by a constable, and there is . . . on his person, or . . . in or on his clothing or footwear, or . . . otherwise in his possession, or . . . in any place in which he is at the time of his arrest, any object, substance or mark, or there is a mark on any such object; and that, or another, constable investigating the case reasonably believes that the presence of the object, substance or mark may be attributable to [their] participation . . . in the commission of the offence specified by the constable; and the constable informs the person arrested that he so believes, and requests him to account

for the presence of the object, substance or mark; and the person fails or refuses to do so, then, if in any proceedings against the person for the offence so specified, evidence on those matters is given.

Under this provision there must be (a) an arrest, (b) an object, substance or mark on any object, (c) that is on their person, in or on their clothing or footwear or in the place of arrest. The arresting officer must (d) reasonably believe that the object, substance or mark on any object might be attributable to the criminal offence with which the accused is charged then (e) inform the accused of that and request that they account for it at the time of arrest and (f) inform the accused of the repercussions of not doing so. Unlike ss 34, 35 and 37 this provision does not require the questioning to take place after the accused has had a chance of obtaining legal advice nor at an authorised place of detention. The court may draw an adverse inference, as they deem proper.

Section 37

The provision states that:

> . . .a person arrested by a constable was found by him at a place at or about the time the offence for which he was arrested is alleged to have been committed . . . and that . . . constable investigating the offence reasonably believes that the presence of the person at that place and at that time may be attributable to his participation in the commission of the offence . . . [he] informs the person that he so believes, and requests him to account for that presence . . . and the person fails or refuses to do so the court or jury, in determining whether the accused is guilty of the offence charged, may draw such inferences from the failure or refusal as appear proper.

You should note that the inference might be drawn after the accused has had a chance to obtain legal advice and it may also vary according to the circumstances of the particular case.

On-the-spot question

 Summarise the requirements of each of the ss 34–37.

CARE WARNINGS

This is a warning that is given by a judge to the jury to take particular care with the evidence of certain witnesses, for instance accomplices, children, those with mental illnesses or victims of sexual offences. The warning will relate to the risk that exists in terms of the evidence of particular witnesses. For instance in the joint trial of Fraser and Siane the trial judge has the discretion to issue a care warning in relation to Fraser's evidence because he may hold a grudge against Siane. Here the evidence of an accomplice must be treated with care because of the potential of a hidden agenda. However, in most cases and where accomplices are concerned, the trial judge has the **discretion** to give the warning but there is no legal requirement to give one (*R v Knowlden* (1981) 77 Cr App R 94 and *R v Bagshaw* [1948] 1 WLR 477).

Section 77 of the PACE Act 1984 states that a trial judge must give a care warning if a **confession** is one made by a mentally handicapped person, where an appropriate adult was not present at the time they made the confession.

EYE AND EARWITNESSES

Eyewitnesses

Often an entire case may rest upon the evidence of an eyewitness. The Devlin Committee investigated the issue in 1976 following a spate of miscarriages of justice that were based on dubious visual identifications. The Court of Appeal took the opportunity to set guidelines in *R v Turnbull* [1977] 3 All ER 549 (CA). In this case Turnbull, along with four other individuals, was separately convicted of conspiracy; his defence was that the eyewitness evidence was mistaken. Two of the appeals were dismissed and two allowed. The guidelines are:

- If the prosecution case is either wholly or substantially based on eyewitness evidence and the defence argues that this is mistaken then the trial judge should warn the jury of the need for caution and the reasons for this.
- Even though the recognition of someone with whom the eyewitness is familiar is of greater reliability than of a stranger, the eyewitness may still make a mistake (*R v Walshe* (1982) 74 Cr App R 85 (CA)).
- Where the eyewitness evidence is of poor quality then the trial judge should withdraw the case from the jury unless other evidence exists that lends support to the identification.
- The jury should be left to assess the weight of good quality eyewitness evidence, however he should give them a warning to be cautious; the trial judge should highlight any evidence that lends support to the identification.

The distinctive features of an accused may render a warning pointless, for example in *R v Slater* [1995] 1 Cr App R 584 the accused was unusually tall and large, the trial judge did not issue a warning and his subsequent appeal was rejected too.

Where the guidelines from *Turnbull* are not followed then it is likely, but not absolute, that the conviction will be quashed on appeal. The conviction may stand if the evidence of the eyewitness forms part of the evidence upon which the conviction is based (*R v Shelton & Carter* [1981] Crim LR 776 (CA)). Where the trial judge is unsure of whether or not to issue a warning then he or she should issue it.

Earwitnesses

Sometimes a witness or jury may be required to compare the voice of an accused with that of a tape or other recording. Like CCTV image analysis this type of evidence requires expert witnesses to analyse it (see *R v Roberts* [2000] Crim LR 183). Voice identification evidence is considered to be more susceptible to mistake than that of eyewitnesses, even though there have been great advances in biometric voice identification technology. The trial judge may choose to issue an appropriate warning to the jury.

On-the-spot question

 What is the rationale for the issue of a Turnbull Warning?

CORROBORATION AND LIES

English law does not require the evidence of witnesses to be corroborated unless provided specifically by statute, for example some speeding offences. The common law required the evidence of some witnesses, for instance children or victims of sexual offences, to be corroborated. The CJA 2003 expressly abolished the common law requirements for corroboration and therefore relevant corroboration warnings (see *R v Makanjuola* (1995) 1 WLR 1348). You should note that often a warning to take caution may still be given where an accomplice runs a cut-throat defence; this is a defence that seeks to strengthen the prosecution case against a co-accused, for example Joyce and Hilary and jointly charged with murder but each claims the other committed the offence.

Lies

A witness may tell lies for a variety of reasons. The basic rule is that a lie cannot corroborate the evidence of a prosecution witness unless certain criteria are satisfied. Figure 6.1 (below) summarises what is required for a lie to corroborate the evidence of a prosecution witness.

If these criteria are established then a lie can amount to evidence in corroboration. The judge may decide to give a Lucas Direction in relation to the significance or the evidence of lies but must make it clear that (a) the evidence is of guilt only if the accused admitted it or if they are sure that the accused lied and (b) they are sure the accused did not lie for an innocent reason. The judge may identify the lie that was told but where there is more than one lie then he or she does not need to list them. A direction should normally be given where the accused has raised an alibi in defence or where the jury may take the lie as evidence of guilt. The Judicial Studies Board (JSB), the organisation that trains magistrates and Crown Court judges in England and Wales, has issued guidelines on what this should include.

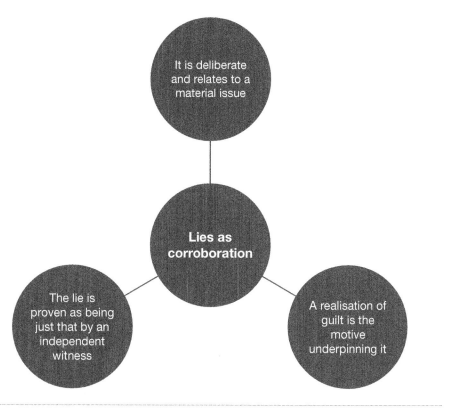

Figure 6.1 Lies as corroboration

KEY CASE ANALYSIS: *R v Lucas* [1981] 2 All ER 1008 CA

In *R v Lucas* [1981] 2 All ER 1008 CA, X (Lucas) and Y were charged with two counts of the importation of cannabis, contrary to the provisions of the Misuse of Drugs Act 1971. Lucas pleaded guilty to count one but not guilty to the other. Z, a prosecution witness, had pleaded guilty and had already been sentenced. Z had proved that X had lied outside of court. The trial judge then directed the jury that this amounted to corroboration. X was convicted and appealed. The Court of Appeal held that evidence of X's lies did not amount to corroboration of the testimony of the prosecution witness. The appeal against conviction was allowed; the court confirmed that there was no real distinction between a lie told in or out of court and gave the following reasoning:

> ... statements made out of court ... which are proved or admitted to be false may ... amount to corroboration ... It accords with good sense that a lie told by a defendant about a material issue may show that the liar knew that if he told the truth he would be sealing his fate ... The jury should in appropriate cases be reminded that people sometimes lie, e.g. in an attempt to bolster up a just cause, or out of shame or ... to conceal disgraceful behaviour.

In *R v Ball* [2001] the court confirmed that a lie, which is central to the issue of a case, would not attract a *Lucas Direction*.

SUMMARY

In English law an accused has the right to remain silent; some inroads have been made into it allowing adverse inferences to be drawn. The right is implied in the right to a fair trial guaranteed by Article 6 of the ECHR. Where eyewitness identification is concerned the trial judge may issue a *Turnbull Warning* requesting the jury to take caution when assessing this evidence because of the risk of mistaken identifications. In general the evidence of a witness does not require corroboration. In terms of lies, a trial judge may choose in certain circumstances to issue a care warning (Lucas Direction) to the jury so as to avoid them using it as evidence of guilt.

FURTHER READING

Bromby, M, MacMillan, M and McKellar, P, 'An examination of criminal jury directions in relation to eyewitness identification in Commonwealth jurisdictions.' (2007) 36(4) CLWR 303.
This article examines the approach on giving directions on the exercise of caution in relation to eyewitness evidence to juries across various commonwealth jurisdictions after the Court of Appeal judgement in *R v Turnbull*.

McConville, M (1993). 'Custodial Legal Advice and the Right to Silence.' London: Her Majesty's Stationery Office.
This is a research study that explores the law and practices on advice and the right to silence.

Pattenden, R, 'Adverse inference from silence: European Court of Human Rights', *Adetoro v United Kingdom* (46834/06). *International Journal of Evidence and Proof*, 2010, 14(3), 272–273.
This is a case comment that considers the ECtHR's judgement in *Adetoro*, which focuses on the right to a fair trial and the right to silence.

Ormerod, D, 'Sounds Familiar? Voice Identification Evidence' [2001] Crim LR 595.
This article explores the issues that surround voice identification evidence.

Chapter 7
Hearsay

LEARNING OUTCOMES

By the end of this chapter, you should be able to:

- Critically engage with the concept of hearsay as evidence
- Understand the principles that relate to the admission of hearsay evidence in civil and criminal proceedings
- Explore the common law and statutory exceptions to the traditional rule against the admission of hearsay as evidence
- Outline the statutory safeguards provided for the admission of hearsay evidence in criminal proceedings

INTRODUCTION

In this chapter the discussion will focus on the admission of hearsay as evidence in civil and criminal proceedings. This will include an exploration of how hearsay is classified and the development of the rules on its admission or exclusion. The focus will then move on to the current statutory regimes for admission in civil and criminal proceedings, the associated risks and relevant safeguards.

HEARSAY – DEFINITION AND EXCLUSION

One of the oldest and fundamental rules in the English law of evidence concerns hearsay. The rule is articulated, inspired by Murphy, as the evidence of a witness that consists of something said by another person, whether orally, in writing or by another method of assertion, for example a gesture on a prior occasion will be inadmissible if it is tendered with the purpose of proving that whatever was stated by the other person on that prior occasion is true. For instance Mark writes to Julia threatening her with legal action if she does not stop writing to him. Julia is found dead two weeks later. At trial for her murder, Mark states that he never knew Julia; the prosecution can tender a letter that he had written her to show that he knew her, rather than as proof that he had threatened her. This highlights that evidence classified as hearsay, where tendered for an alterative purpose, something other than to prove the truth of its contents, will be admissible. You should note that the normal rules on relevance and admissibility apply. Figure 7.1 summarises the rule:

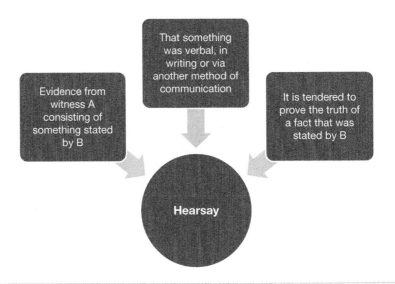

Figure 7.1 Hearsay definition

There are a number of criticisms of hearsay evidence. The first is that the evidence of the other person cannot be properly tested by cross-examination as they did not 'perceive' that which they are giving evidence in relation to personally. The second is that witnesses may make errors when recalling the statement that was made. Another reason was that it was not perceived to be the best form of evidence (see *Teper v R* [1952] AC 480 and Chapter 1).

There was a school of thought that suggested that the jury attaching the appropriate amount of weight to the evidence through judicial direction could mitigate the risk. In its report 'Evidence in Criminal Proceedings: Hearsay and Related Topics' the Law Commission propounded the need for reform to this area of evidence law; this will be discussed later.

In criminal proceedings, prior to the changes made by the CJA 2003, a mixture of common law, statutory provisions and practical application governed the rules on hearsay. The roots of the rule against the admission of hearsay evidence, which applied to examination-in-chief, cross-examination and re-examination, were firmly rooted in the common law (see *R v Blastland* [1986] AC 41).

KEY CASE ANALYSIS: *Sparks v R* [1964] AC 964

Background

The evidence of the mother of a victim of an assault sought to give evidence that her daughter had described the assailant as a black man was inadmissible because it was hearsay. The evidence, had it been admitted, would have resulted in the defendant – who incidentally was a white male – being acquitted.

Principle established

Sparks highlights how strictly the rule was applied and therefore a number of exceptions to it developed in the common law, something later curtailed by the House of Lords in *DPP v Myers* [1965] AC 1001.

On-the-spot question

Summarise the elements of the hearsay rule.

What was the rationale for excluding hearsay evidence?

The current definition of a hearsay statement, for the purposes of criminal proceedings, is outlined in s 115(2) as '. . . any representation of fact or opinion made by a person by whatever means . . . [including] a representation made in a sketch, photofit or other pictorial form.' To decipher whether a statement is hearsay, ask yourself the following questions:

- Is this a statement, assertion or a gesture that was made out of court by another person?
- What is it being tendered to prove?
- If it is tendered as the truth of its contents then, did the person who made the statement intend others to act upon or believe it?

THE CIVIL EVIDENCE ACT 1995

Hearsay has been admissible in English civil proceedings for many years; the Civil Evidence Act 1995 was specifically enacted for this purpose and thus the approach has been one of inclusion rather than exclusion.

THE CRIMINAL JUSTICE ACT 2003

The Criminal Justice Act 2003 (CJA) introduced a major change to the traditional exclusionary approach in criminal proceedings, thereby modernising the law; the approach is now inclusionary (*R v Joyce and Joyce* [2005] EWCA Crim 1785). Hearsay evidence is now admissible in all stages of criminal proceedings (**newton hearings**, the trial stage and sentencing) provided it falls into one of the categories provided in the CJA 2003.

Admissibility

Section 114 of the CJA 2003 provides that:

> . . . a statement not made in oral evidence in the proceedings is admissible as evidence of any matter stated if, but only if . . . any provision of this Chapter or any other statutory provision makes it admissible . . . any rule of law preserved by Section 118 makes it admissible . . . all parties to the proceedings agree to it being admissible . . . [or] the court is satisfied that it is in the interests of justice for it to be admissible.

Section 115(2) of the CJA 2003 defines a hearsay statement as any representation of fact or opinion that is made by a person by any means including pictorial form, photofit and a sketch. The implication is that statements produced by mechanical processes, for instance videos do not fall within it and thus admission for those should be sought via alternative means.

Section 115(3) of the CJA 2003 provides a definition of what amounts to a matter stated as '. . . the purpose, or one of the purposes, of the person making the statement appears to the court to have been . . . to cause another [person] to believe it or act [upon it] or a machine to operate on the basis that the matter is as stated.'

The court must consider a number of factors when deciding upon admission in the interests of justice under s 114(1)(d) of the CJA 2003, under s 114(2), these include:

> . . .how much probative value the statement has (assuming it to be true) in relation to a matter in issue in the proceedings, or how valuable it is for the

understanding of other evidence in the case . . . what other evidence has been, or can be, given on the matter or evidence . . . how important the matter or evidence is in the context of the case as a whole . . . the circumstances in which the statement was made . . . how reliable the maker of the statement appears to be . . . how reliable the evidence of the making of the statement appears to be . . . whether oral evidence of the matter stated can be given and, if not, why it cannot . . . the amount of difficulty involved in challenging the statement . . . the extent to which that difficulty would be likely to prejudice the party facing it.

This provision is said to contain the safety values under which hearsay is admissible under such a wide discretion to admit. You should note that the judge is not required to ascertain an answer for all of these (see *R v Taylor* [2006] 2 Cr App R 14).

Extent

The rules apply to any assertions, gestures and statements made by someone on a prior occasion. In *Chandrasekera v R* [1937] AC 220 the victim had her throat cut but the court accepted the gestures (nodding head and the signs she made with her hands) she made shortly before she succumbed to her injuries as admissible evidence. The evidence of witnesses in their interpretation of what she meant by the signs was inadmissible hearsay. You should note that hearsay statements can be positive, for example that Francis has done something, but also negative, for instance Surinder has not done something (see *DPP v Leigh* [2010] EWHC 345 (Admin)).

In *Myers v DPP* [1965] AC 1001 the court held that the evidence the prosecution sought to adduce from car manufacturers of the detailed information they kept that related to secret chassis numbers to prove that the cars the accused had were in fact stolen was inadmissible hearsay evidence. You should note that on appeal the court held this to be evidence that carried a special quality in its own right because it was peculiar.

Previous inconsistent statements also fall under this category (s 119 of the CJA 2003) as truth of the matters they state; in order for them to be admissible the maker is called to give oral evidence. Prior to this a previous inconsistent statement was only admitted as evidence that undermined the maker's credibility. Section 119 of the Criminal Procedure Act 1865 must still be satisfied for the admission of this statement as evidence; this means the statement must first be mentioned to the maker of it and then questioned as to whether they made it. Equally, previous consistent statements can be adduced to rebut an allegation that the maker has fabricated their evidence. This is clearly hearsay. In definition the condition is that oral evidence of the same matter should have been admissible under the normal rules. A witness may use a previous statement to refresh their memory while giving evidence but this will result in that statement being admissible as evidence of the truth of any fact it contains (see s 120 CJA 2003). You should note that there is no rule of law that prevents a witness from refreshing his or her memory from any document that they made prior to trial; the criticism of this is that the witness's evidence is most likely to be affected by doing this.

Purpose

Classification as hearsay depends upon the purpose for which evidence is tendered, for example Debbie crashes into Filipe's car, she gets out and runs towards Filipe shouting, 'I'm going to kill you,' and then punches Filipe in the face causing him to suffer a fractured skull. Debbie begins to walk off. Jean sees Debbie walking away and runs over to Filipe; before he succumbs to his injuries he points to Debbie and tells Jean: 'It was her who killed me.' When the police arrive (called by another witness) Jean runs over and tells them that she is willing to tell the court everything. A statement such as this if tendered to prove the truth of its contents – namely that Debbie killed Filipe – is clearly hearsay and therefore would need to satisfy the CJA 2003 or the common law before it could be admitted. In *R v Attard* (1858) 43 Cr App R 90 the evidence of a police officer, that consisted of what the interpreter had told the officer what the accused had said, was inadmissible hearsay evidence. In *Teper v R* [1952] AC 480 the evidence of a witness who had heard someone shouting something at another person was held to be inadmissible hearsay, even though the statement that was heard incriminated the accused and destroyed his alibi. Statements that are adduced for reasons other than to prove the truth of their contents can be classed as original evidence (see Chapter 1). For instance, if Jean's evidence were adduced to prove that Filipe made a statement before he died or to prove what Filipe's state of mind was at the time, it would not be subject to the rules on the exclusion of hearsay evidence. What follows is a summary of some of the categories of original evidence.

Evidence of the fact that a statement was made

The court may allow a statement that would otherwise be classed as hearsay to be tendered to prove the fact that it was made rather than to prove the truth of its contents. In *Subramaniam v Public Prosecutor* [1956] 1 WLR 965 the Privy Council permitted the admission of a statement to prove that threats had been made to the accused and what effect they had had on him. In *Woodhouse v Hall* (1980) 72 Cr App R 39 the evidence of officers that various women had offered them sexual services while they were at a massage parlour was admissible as original evidence that circumstantially proved that the accused was running a brothel.

Evidence of the mind of the maker or recipient of a statement at the time it was made

Statements may be adduced to prove what the state of mind was of the maker or recipient of a statement. In *Jones v DPP* [1962] AC 635 and *Mawaz Khan and Amanat Khan v R* [1967] AC 454 the courts respectively held that evidence of false alibis was admissible to prove that an accused had a guilty mind.

KEY CASE ANALYSIS: *R v Kearley* [1992] 2 All ER 345

Background

Evidence of the telephone and physical calls of various people to Kearley's home requesting to purchase drugs was intercepted by the police during a search they were carrying out while he was not home. This was admitted as evidence to prove that Kearley was selling drugs. The prosecution sought to prove that the calls themselves amounted to an implied assertion that he was.

Principle established

He was convicted and appealed; the House of Lords decided that this implied assertion (a statement that infers a fact) was inadmissible hearsay evidence. The fact that calls had been made and the state of mind of the callers was not in itself a fact in issue for the purposes of the commission of the offence. The fact that the callers thought they could obtain drugs was irrelevant; the result of admission would lead a jury to believe that the premises were being used to sell drugs. The house distinguished the decision in *Woodhouse* on the basis that the offer in that case (the offer of sexual services) was made by an employee; here Kearley had not contacted the individuals.

In *R v Singh* [2006] 1 WLR 1564 the Court of Appeal has confirmed that an implied assertion is not hearsay evidence and therefore does not need to satisfy the requirements of the CJA 2003. In *R v Twist and Others* [2011] EWCA Crim 1143 the Court of Appeal has recommended that the 'implied assertion' be avoided because the scheme for exclusion under the CJA 2003 concentrates on 'matters stated'. The court considered that the court should ask itself these questions: (a) what matter is the statement looking to prove? (b) is reference to that matter made in the statement? If the answer to this latter question is no, then the statement is not hearsay. If, however, the answer is yes, the court should decide whether the maker of the statement wished for the recipient to believe it was true or act on it. If the answer to the latter question is a further yes, then it is hearsay evidence and the

CJA 2003 scheme applies. The questions satisfy the general requirements for hearsay to have been made out of court and tendered to prove the truth of its contents.

Subramaniam highlights that evidence of the effect that a statement has on the mind of the statement's recipient is admissible; it is not hearsay because it is not being tendered for the truth of its contents.

Records

Records are normally admitted as documentary evidence (see Chapter 1). In terms of hearsay, records present a peculiar problem: whether no record can amount to an assertion that no reply was received. In *DPP v Leigh* [2010] EWHC 345 (Admin) Leigh was the registered keeper of a car and was charged with failing to supply information on the identity of the driver caught speeding in his car on two previous occasions. The witness gave evidence that Leigh had not replied on either of the two occasions. The court held that this evidence was not hearsay, confirming that the non-existence of a record where one was normally expected to exist was a fact and not a statement. The court highlighted that it would be fictitious to take the non-existence of a record where one was normally expected to exist as being a statement. Evidence of the non-existence of the record given by the witness would be direct evidence. The case affirms the position of the common and statutory law as outlined in *R v Patel* (1981) 73 Cr App R 117; *R v Shone* (1982) 76 Cr App R 72 and s 115(3) of the CJA 2003, subject to the requirement that the witness must give first-hand evidence of the process by which the record is compiled. You should note that records that are produced by machines but where there is human input, namely that someone enters the data, will be classed as hearsay evidence. This is currently admissible under s 129(1) and (2) of the CJA 2003; the provision also presumes that the technology is in good working order.

Documentary Evidence

Prior to ss 116 and 117 of the CJA 2003, ss 23 and 24 of the CJA 1988 (CJA) provided for the admission of documentary hearsay evidence where it was not possible to adduce the witness at trial. Under s 116(1) of the CJA 2003, first-hand documentary and oral hearsay evidence is admissible provided that evidence would have been admissible had the witness been available to give evidence at trial, the court is satisfied as to who made the statement and either one of the conditions in s 116(2)(a)–(e) is satisfied, that is, the maker of the statement:

- is dead or mentally or physically unfit;
- cannot be found after all reasonable attempts have been made to try and find them;
- is outside the United Kingdom and therefore their attendance cannot be practicably or reasonably secured; or

Sections 116(2)(a)–(e) of the CJA 2003	Detail
Death, mentally or physically unfit	The party seeking admission must prove this.
Not possible to secure attendance	The party seeking admission must prove this (*R v Radak* [1999] 1 Cr App R 187). They must take all reasonable steps to secure the attendance.
Does not give or continue to give oral evidence	Fear includes death, financial loss or injury to themselves or others (*R v Davies (Anita)* [2006] EWCA Crim 2643). The court must give leave for the statement to be adduced.

Figure 7.2 Conditions for the admission of hearsay

- is in fear and does not give or continue to give evidence and the court gives leave for the statement to be given.

Under this provision such a statement is admissible as proof of any fact that the witness would have been eligible to give oral evidence in relation to at trial (*Sparks v R* [1964] AC 964). Where any of the first three provisions apply the statement will be automatically admissible, in terms of the latter the court must give leave for it to be admitted. Figure 7.2 outlines the law in relation to each of these:

KEY CASE ANALYSIS: *R v O'Loughlin* [1988] 3 All ER 431

Background

The accused had been threatened not to give evidence by some terrorists. The court confirmed that, where the party is seeking to adduce hearsay because the witness does not give evidence through fear, they must prove that through evidence that is admissible.

Principle established

Where an application for admission is made, the court would decide whether to admit the statement by asking itself this question: would a reasonable person have suffered the fear had they been in that position (objective test). In considering whether the statement should be admitted the court will have regard under s 116(4) to:

- what the statement contains;
- any risk that its admission or exclusion would result in unfairness to either party if the statement is excluded;
- any special measures directions that could be made under ss 17 and 19 of the Youth Justice and Public Order Act 1999;
- that the evidence will not be tested through cross-examination; and
- any other circumstances.

Sections 117(1) and (2) of the CJA 2003 provide, in relation to business or other documents, that:

> . . . a statement contained in a document is admissible as evidence of any matter stated if . . . oral evidence given in the proceedings would be admissible as evidence of that matter . . . [and [a]] the document or the part containing the statement was created or received by a person in the course of a trade, business, profession or other occupation, or as the holder of a paid or unpaid office . . . [b] the person who supplied the information contained in the statement (the relevant person) had or may reasonably be supposed to have had personal knowledge of the matters dealt with [and they may [c]] . . . reasonably be supposed [to have] received the information in the course of a trade, business, profession or other occupation, or as the holder of a paid or unpaid office.

All three conditions must be satisfied. You will notice that the requirement for the statement to be created in the course of a trade, business, profession or other occupation so as to afford it a degree of reliability. There is no need under this provision for the person tendering the statement to prove that the person who created the statement is not available to give evidence (see *R v Foxley* [1995] 2 Cr App R 523).

Section 117(4) of the CJA 2003 allows for the admission of documents that have been prepared for litigation that is contemplated or pending. The requirements of ss 117(1)–(2) and s 117(5) must also be satisfied in order to achieve this; these are that the maker of the statement:

- is mentally or physically unfit or dead;
- cannot be found after all reasonable attempts have been made to try and find them;
- is outside of the United Kingdom and therefore their attendance cannot be practicably or reasonably secured;
- is in fear and does not give or continue to give evidence and the court gives leave for the statement to be given;

- cannot reasonably be expected to have any recollection of the matters dealt with in the statement (having regard to the length of time since he supplied the information and all other circumstances).

These are the same requirements as those under s 116(2)(a)–(e), with the addition of the latter namely the length of time that has elapsed between the making the statement and the proceedings. The provision only applies to anyone who makes the statement. This is clearly an issue relating to reliability but also common sense. The new provisions are clearer than the predecessor's ss 23 and 24 of the CJA 1988.

Sections 117(6) and (7) of the CJA 2003 state that a statement is not admissible if the court:

> is satisfied that the statement's reliability as evidence for the purpose for which it is tendered is doubtful in view of . . . its contents, the source of the information contained in it . . . the way in which or the circumstances in which the information was supplied or received, or the way in which or the circumstances in which the document concerned was created or received.

Multiple hearsay

This is hearsay that passes from one party to another prior to being recorded. Such evidence is admissible as a business document (s 117 of the CJA 2003) or as a previous consistent or inconsistent statement (ss 119 and 120 of the CJA 2003) or where all parties or the court of its own accord decide to admit it (s 121).

THE COMMON LAW EXCEPTIONS

The CJA 2003 expressly preserves a number of the common law exceptions that allowed the admission of hearsay as evidence (see s 118). Figure 7.3 (below) summarises these.

What follows is a brief summary of each one.

Admissions, common enterprise and confessions

A confession or admission whether wholly or partly adverse to its maker or by their agent is admissible as prove of the truth of its contents regardless of whether it was made through conduct, orally or in writing. An agent for these purposes may be the lawyer who is instructed to act on the accused's behalf and the admission must be made in line with the instructions and to the opposition without any fraud. The statement must consist of

Figure 7.3 Hearsay: the common law exceptions under the CJA 2003

something that is within the maker's knowledge and not hearsay, for example 'Joan forced me to do it': this will be reliable because it is incriminatory. However, if the maker of the statement states 'Joan made me do it' and Joan is present and says nothing then the statement will be admissible as evidence of Joan's non-reaction. Perhaps this does not take into account that people may confess to crimes they did not commit for many reasons, for instance passion or coercion (see *R v Vasiliki Pryce and Christopher Huhne* (2013), unreported).

In civil proceedings such an admission statement is admissible under the Civil Evidence Act 1995; in criminal proceedings the matter is governed by s 76 of the PACE Act 1984 and s 118 of the CJA 2003. In terms of the latter the jury will attribute appropriate weight to it by assessing the entire statement and taking into account any explanations it may have contained, for instance Maite may confess to assaulting Xavier but that she did so in self-defence.

In civil proceedings, an admission made by A that implicates B is admissible under the Civil Evidence Act 1995 however in criminal proceedings a confession will only bind its maker unless A and B are jointly accused for the commission of an offence. The requirement is that statement was made while the offence, one of joint enterprise, was being carried out.

The rule is strict; thus if A makes the statement that also incriminates B after the offence has been committed then it will only bind A (see *R v Blake* (1844) 115 ER 49).

Public documents

The contents of a document that is public, namely a document that is not confidential and is available to the public at large whether generally or on request, is admissible as proof of the truth of its contents. The common law on the admission of documents set out a number of requirements prior to their admission that included the contemporaneous (to the event it sought to document) creation of a document for public record, its contents were required to be of public interest and inspection, and the person who created it was required to have some personal knowledge of the manner in which it was made. The exception developed on the rationale that public documents go through a lot of scrutiny and therefore there was no requirement that its creator verify that the process was rigorous. This also meant that the accused could challenge the document on the basis that its production was flawed in some way. Section 118(1)(b) of the CJA 2003 preserved this common law exception as it is.

Res gestae

In criminal proceedings a hearsay statement that is made as part of the res gestae (state of affairs) is admissible as evidence to prove the truth of its contents. Sections 114(1)(d) and 118(1)(4) of the CJA 2003 have preserved this common law exception and the law accompanying it. There are two conditions that must be satisfied: (a) the statement must be made spontaneously and (b) it must form an integral part of the event. The logic is that the statement almost forms part of the event because it is inherent to it and the risk of fabrication is mitigated by the spontaneity by which it is made (*Thompson v Trevanion*, Holt 286; K.B. 1693). Philip, in Ealing High Street, attacks Malcolm, who runs into a store where he meets a policeman to whom he relays everything that has happened. Donley has seen the entire episode. The statement Malcolm makes to the policeman will be admissible as evidence forming part of the res gestae to prove the truth of its contents and Malcolm's contemporaneous state of mind. If Donley makes the statement then it must be treated with caution. The fact that Malcolm has made the statement after the event does not affect its spontaneity, the House of Lords confirmed in *R v Andrews* [1987] AC 251 that in admitting a statement that was made after the event the court should ask itself whether the maker of the statement had had the opportunity to reflect upon what had happened and whether the event still dominated their mind. Thus, if Malcolm drove home and then telephoned the police in a frightened and shaken state the likelihood is that his statement would be admissible under this exception (see also *Ratten v R* [1972] AC 378). *Andrews* overrules the absurdity in cases such as *R v Bedingfield* (1879) 14 Cox CC 341 where the victims statement was inadmissible because it was made shortly after the event – in this case the victim had had her throat slit and the statement was made by her after she managed to get out of the room where she had been attacked. You should note that the common law exception that permitted a statement made by a person who is since deceased was abolished by the CJA 2003 but may be admissible under s 116(2)(a) of the 2003 Act (discussed later).

Res gestae: a statement that evidences the maker's mental or physical state

The law on this point is best evidenced by an example. Anthony makes a statement to Peter that he has been very poorly and that he is sure that his wife Kathryn is trying to kill him. If Anthony dies then his statement to Peter may be admissible as evidence to prove that (a) Kathryn was trying to kill him or (b) that he was feeling poorly. The first is clearly hearsay and thus the normal rules must apply but the second can be tendered to evidence his poor health (see *Gilbey v Great Western Railway* (1910) 102 LT 202). The requirement is that reference must be made to the maker of the statement's poor health and not that of another (see also *R v Conde* (1867) 10 Cox CC 547).

Statutory exceptions

You should note that a number of other statutes also provide exceptions to the hearsay rule, these include:

* The Children and Young Persons Act 1933
* The Criminal Justice Act 1988
* Youth Justice and Criminal Evidence Act 1999.

On-the-spot questions

What is the rationale that underpins the decision in Kearley?

In what instance is the confession of A admissible as evidence against B?

Explain what is meant by the term res gestae.

Safeguards

Sections 124–126 of the CJA 2003 and s 78 of the PACE Act 1984 provide safeguards in relation to the admission of hearsay evidence. Figure 7.4 summarises their impact:

Each of these safeguards focuses on the risks attached to the admission of such evidence.

Human rights

This aspect of the law pervades the various areas of law. The right to a fair trial under Article 6 of the ECHR includes the right of the defence to be able to challenge the evidence through cross-examination. The safeguards, as discussed, provide some protection in terms of this. The main sticking point from the jurisprudence of the ECtHR seems to be related to the instance in which a prosecution is substantially based on hearsay evidence as a result of which the defence's ability to challenge it is restricted. The rules under the CJA 2003 provide for this, so this situation should ideally be avoided.

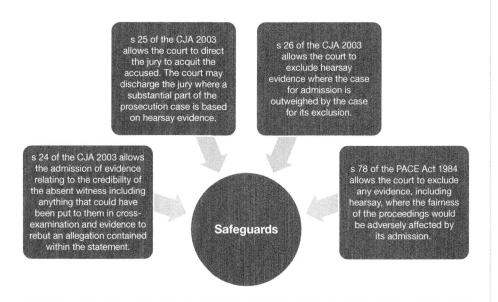

Figure 7.4 Safeguards

On-the-spot questions

What is the rationale that underpins the need for safeguards when admitting hearsay evidence?

What is the extent or impact of the protection provided by the safeguards on hearsay evidence that is adduced at trial under one of the provisions of the CJA 2003?

SUMMARY

Hearsay is a popular assessment topic and one that has a basis in statutory and common law. The rules seek to balance the admission of evidence and the particular risks associated with it. The approach on the admission of hearsay in both criminal and civil proceedings in English law is an inclusionary one. Evidence, even hearsay, where tendered for an alterative purpose may be admissible under the rules that accompany the admission of that type of evidence, for example as proof of lies etc.

FURTHER READING

Hirst, M, 'Interpreting the new concept of hearsay'. [2010] CLJ 69(1) 72.
This article focuses on whether the changes to the admission of hearsay evidence brought around by the CJA 2003 through a fair, redefined and clarified set of rules have been effective.

Malek, HM, Auburn, J and Bagshaw, R (eds) (2012). *Phipson on Evidence*, 17th edn. London: Sweet & Maxwell.
This is the reference text on the law of evidence for students, academics and practitioners alike. The text is useful for detailed reference to some of the more obscure areas of evidence law.

Landa, CS (2012). *Evidence: Question and Answers 2013–2014*, 10th edn. London: Routledge.
This textbook focuses on the application of the law of evidence with some interesting practical questions and guidance on answering assessment questions.

Mirfield, P, 'A Final Farewell to Kearley.' (2012) LQR 128(Jul) 331.
This case comment relates to the decision in *Kearley and R v Twist (Andrew Terence) and others* [2011] EWCA Crim 1143 and the effect of the CJA 2003 on hearsay and implied assertions.

Chapter 8
Confessions and other evidence

LEARNING OUTCOMES

By the end of this chapter, you should be able to:

- Critically engage with the principles that relate to confession evidence
- Understand and evaluate the rules on the admission or exclusion of confession evidence and their purpose and effect
- Determine the rules on other unlawfully obtained evidence for example the agent provocateur

INTRODUCTION

The discussion in this chapter focuses on confession evidence. This includes a brief look at what amounts to a confession in law and the rules on the admission or exclusion of this evidence at trial. The discussion then shifts to the rules that govern other evidence that is obtained unlawfully.

CONFESSIONS

The English law on confessions has developed in the common law but there is a variety of supporting measures for the PACE Act 1984 and the COP 2012 that accompany it. Confessions are statements, whether in words or otherwise, that are wholly or partly adverse to the person that made it and regardless of whether that was made to a person in authority or otherwise. A confession is relevant to the accused's guilt as an exception to the hearsay rule (see Chapter 7); notions of freedom from oppression and voluntariness in confessing is still very much at the heart of the current law (see *Ibrahim v R* [1914] AC 599 and *R v Priestly* (1965) 51 Cr App R1).

Figure 8.1 summarises the law and rules upon which confession evidence is currently governed, these are:

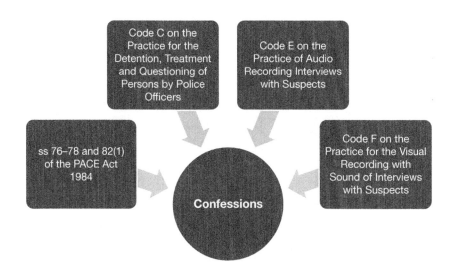

Figure 8.1 Confession evidence under English law

The purpose of the 1984 Act was to bring together policing powers and practices and to establish a much needed balance between the police and the communities they serve. The COP that accompany the PACE Act 1984 are not rules of law but Codes that guide the police in the conduct of a range of necessary procedures in policing and the lawful extent of their powers. The COP apply to all those individuals who are involved in the investigation of offences or with charging people that may have committed criminal offences. The police clearly fall within this definition as do customs officers and security guards (see s 67(9) of the PACE Act 1984 and *R v Gill* [2004] 1 WLR 469). Breaches of the COP may result in the evidence, including confession evidence, being excluded from admission (discussed later).

Defining a confession

Section 82(1) of the PACE Act 1984 defines a confession as '. . . any statement that is wholly or partly adverse to the person who made it . . . whether made to a person in authority or not and whether made in words or otherwise.' This definition caused a number of problems for the courts in terms of how it could be interpreted. The provision allows a mixed statement, namely one that is not wholly adverse to the maker, to be admitted as a confession. The requirement that the statement be adverse must be satisfied at the time the statement is made (see *R v Sat-Bhambra* (1988) 88 Cr App R 55). Statements made by the maker that are favourable to them will not fall under this provision (*R v Sat-Bhambra* (above) and *R v Park* [1994] 99 Cr App R 270). Neither will statements that are favourable to the accused at the time they are made but that later become adverse.

Other than the form of the statement for which there are no requirements (for example a confession may appear as a tweet on Twitter, a post on Facebook or a video on YouTube) there are however a number of other considerations to which you should have regard. The first is that the content of the statement must be clear. For example Donley on being arrested at the scene of a crime says 'sods law'; such a statement will not amount to a confession (see *R v Schofield* (1917) 12 Cr App R 191). Second, the provision does not require the statement to have been made to someone in a position of authority and therefore Mark may confess to his mother, Theresa, that he assaulted Ursula.

A confession statement will not be presented to court as a document that states verbatim what was said. Instead it will be a narrative summary of the most salient points including those remarks that indict the accused and those that exonerate them.

Admission and exclusion – ss 76 and 76A of the PACE Act 1984

In order for a statement to be admitted as a confession, where it has satisfied the above requirements, it should have been obtained in a lawful manner that complies with COP C and E of the PACE Act 1984 (see also Code F on the visual recording (with sound) of police interviews). The general rule is that a confession is only admissible as evidence of guilt against its maker and in English law such evidence does not need to be corroborated. You should remember that the trial judge has the discretion under s 78 of the PACE Act 1984 to exclude the admission of any evidence, having regard to all the circumstances in which it was obtained, which has an adverse effect on the fairness of the proceedings.

As evidence of the guilt of the accused

Section 76(1) states '. . . a confession made by an accused person may be given in evidence against him in so far as it is relevant to any matter in issue in the proceedings and is not excluded by the court in pursuance of this section'. Section 76(2) provides a safeguard; it states:

> . . . where the prosecution proposes to give in evidence a confession made by an accused person, it is represented to the court that the confession was or may have been obtained (a) by oppression of the person who made it; or (b) in consequence of anything said or done which was likely, in the circumstances existing at the time, to render unreliable any . . . confession which might be made by him in consequence thereof . . . the court shall not allow the confession to be given in evidence against him except in so far as the prosecution proves to the court beyond reasonable doubt that the confession (notwithstanding that it may be true) was not obtained as aforesaid.

Section 76(8) defines oppression as 'torture, inhuman or degrading treatment, and the use or threat of violence (whether or not amounting to torture)'. Therefore, a confession may be excluded where it is obtained by oppression or where things said or done mean it is unreliable. The difficulties in defining the term 'oppression' has produced a lot of case law, for instance in *R v Fulling* [1987] QB 426 the Court of Appeal held that the police telling the accused that her partner was having an affair, after which she confessed to having committed the crime, did not amount to oppression. The current law requires that the oppression by someone in a position of authority, for instance a police officer, caused the accused to confess to having committed the offence. Oppression includes degrading or inhumane treatment and torture (see *A and Others v Secretary of State for the Home Department (No.2)* [2006] 2 AC 231).

KEY CASE ANALYSIS: *R v Miller, Paris and Others* (1993) 97 Cr App R 99

Background

The court found that the police had obtained a confession by oppression from an accused who had a retarded mental age, after he was subjected to verbal bullying and over 13 hours of interviewing during which he was refused access to legal advice and he denied involvement over 300 times.

Principle established

These factors would normally render a confession unlawful by reason of oppression where the accused is not mentally retarded. The case highlights what amounts to oppression but not the point at which the police cross the fine line and their questioning then becomes oppressive.

A confession can also be excluded because it was obtained by things said or done, which were likely, in the circumstances at the time, to render it unreliable (s 76(2)(b)). The provision covers those instances in which conduct may fall short of amounting to oppression. The following two conditions must be satisfied if a confession is to be excluded under this provision: first, things must be said or done – these can be acts or omissions but must be extraneous (external) to the subject. Second, those things when put in the context of the specific circumstances at that time must cause the accused to confess; this will then render the confession unreliable (see *R v Goldenberg* [1988] Crim LR 678). The test in considering the specific circumstances at that time is objective, for instance characteristics peculiar to the defendant, such as drug or alcohol addictions, are irrelevant. However, the courts have deviated from this test by taking into account characteristics such as mental incapacity regardless of the fact that in those authorities a number of factors existed that would have rendered the confession unreliable (see *R v Everett* [1988] Crim LR 826 and *R v Blackburn* [2005] EWCA Crim 1349). In *R v Harvey* [1988] Crim LR 241 the court excluded the confession of an accused who was mentally retarded and had confessed to a murder in the presence of her lesbian lover. The pressure put on the accused by the presence of the latter rendered it unreliable. In *R v McGovern* (1990) 92 Cr App R 228 a confession by a heavily pregnant woman was rendered unreliable because she was highly emotive by reason of her pregnancy, mentally retarded and she had been denied the opportunity to obtain legal advice.

Finally there must be a causal link between the oppression and unreliability with the act of the accused confessing. Therefore, if the oppression or things said or done are no longer operative when the confession is made, then causation will not be established. This means that the oppression or things said or done must be fairly contemporaneous with the making of the confession.

You should note that under s 76(3) the court may, of its own accord, require the prosecution to prove that a confession was not obtained by oppression or by things said or done that render the confession inadmissible. Section 76(4) provides that the whole or part exclusion of a confession does not affect the admissibility of any facts that are discovered as a result of the confession having been made or that the accused is able to express themselves by speaking, writing or in another way. In terms of the former, after being questioned for hours without a break, food or water, Mabel confesses to having stolen the Picasso painting from the gallery. The painting is subsequently recovered from her attic. If her confession becomes inadmissible because of the manner in which it was obtained then the evidence recovered as a result of it (the painting) is still admissible. Where such evidence is admitted then the prosecution is not permitted to refer to how it was discovered (s 76(5)); the only person who can reveal this is the accused.

You should note that, where possible, the party seeking to adduce the statement may edit it to remove the offending parts so that they are then able to present it as evidence supporting the facts discovered as a result of it, or to prove that the accused can express him- or herself in any way including by speaking and writing (s 76(4) of the PACE Act 1984). Figure 8.2 (below) summarises the effect of editing a confession in terms of remarks that exonerate or indict an accused:

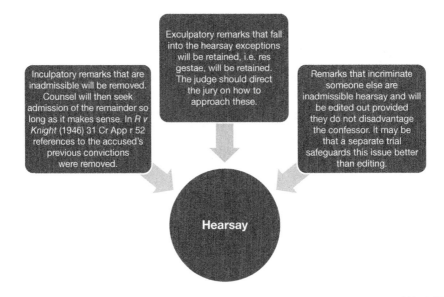

Figure 8.2 Editing confessions

Confessions as evidence of the guilt of a co-accused

Section 76A provides that a confession may be given in evidence for a co-accused charged in the same proceedings provided it is relevant to a matter in issue and the court does not exclude it. Where an accused wishes to adduce the confession of a co-accused, the court must be satisfied that it was not obtained through '. . . oppression of the person who made it, or . . . in consequence of anything said or done, which was likely, in the circumstances existing at the time, to render unreliable any confession which might be made by him in consequence thereof.' Where it is proven that the confession was not obtained in that manner then it will be included (s 76A(2)). Under s 76A(3) the court may decide of its own motion that it must be proven on balance of probabilities that the confession was not so obtained. Again, evidence that is obtained from a wholly or partly excluded confession will be admissible of any facts that are discovered as a result of the confession having been made or that the accused is able to express themselves by speaking, writing or in another way. Where such evidence is admitted then the co-accused is not permitted to refer to how it was discovered (s 76A(5)); only the accused can reveal this.

KEY CASE ANALYSIS: *R v Myers* [1997] 3 WLR 552

Background

A and B were charged with murder; both blamed one another for the commission of the crime. A made two confessions and in both she admitted stabbing the victim so that she could rob him. At trial A denied making the confessions and the prosecution did not adduce them as evidence of A's guilt. B adduced A's confessions in defence. A appealed on the basis that the confession were inadmissible.

Principle established

The House of Lords decided against A; the confessions were admissible because they were relevant to B's defence.

Confessions by the mentally handicapped

There is, quite rightly, additional protection in relation to confessions for those individuals that are mentally handicapped. Section 77 of the PACE Act 1984 requires the confession to have been made in the presence of an independent person; the independence of that person is important to promote fairness, as the case of *R v Harvey* [1988] Crim LR 241 highlights. Lawyers, police officers and other persons in a similar capacity are specifically excluded from acting as an independent person in such a case (s 77(3)). The decision of the court in *R v J* [2003] EWCA Crim 3309 demonstrates that the trial judge should warn the jury to exercise caution when convicting such a person on the basis of a confession. Further it also outlines that a breach of these provisions will render a confession inadmissible as evidence.

Weight

Once the confession is admitted as evidence, the jury will assess how much weight to attribute to it; this is deciphered by the following question: to what extent do we believe it to be true, taking into account the entirety of the circumstances. The quality of the evidence, in the jury's mind, would be affected by the arguments legal counsel – whether for the prosecution, defence or co-accused – makes in relation to the purpose for which it is being adduced, for example as evidence of guilt or in support of an accused's defence that they were coerced into doing something they would not have otherwise done. You should note that there is no right of appeal based on the fact that the jury gave a confession more weight than it should have.

Risks associated with confession evidence

Sections 76 and 76A reveal that confession evidence is regarded with caution because people may admit things for a number of reasons, including duress (threats of violence), fabrication or undue influence, for instance marital coercion and mental disability. Counsel for the maker of the statement (the confessor) may challenge the existence, factual basis or content of a confession. For instance Dirk is charged with manslaughter. His girlfriend Pansy was found lying dead at the bottom of the stairs in the flat that they both shared. On questioning by the police Dirk makes a statement that includes the following adverse content: 'I never meant for her to die'; the prosecution argues that this amounts to a confession. Counsel for Dirk argues that the statement is not evidence of guilt because it referred to Dirk's tumultuous relationship with Pansy and an argument that they had had prior to her death, therefore it is not reasonable for the jury to conclude that he is guilty. Note: you should assume that reference to these latter points had been made in Dirk's examination-in-chief and loosely in the statement he had made to the police; therefore considerations of adverse inferences etc. do not apply.

Other than the instance in which an accused denies making a confession, his or her counsel will normally make an application to exclude a confession in a **voir dire**, that is, a trial within a trial (*Ajodha v The State* [1982] AC 204). This is a procedure that is undertaken in absence of the jury. During this procedure the accused can give evidence but should be aware that the prosecution may use any evidence that emerges if the confession is subsequently deemed admissible (*Wong Kam Ming v R* [1980] AC 247).

On-the-spot questions

What is the purpose of adducing a confession at trial?

How is weight attributed to a confession?

On what basis may counsel challenge a confession?

Summarise the instances in which the court may exclude a confession.

EXCLUSION OF UNFAIR EVIDENCE – S 78 OF THE PACE ACT 1984

This provision gives the court a broad discretion, which runs alongside the courts more limited common law discretion, to exclude any evidence on which:

> . . . the prosecution proposes to rely . . . if it appears to the court that, having regard to all the circumstances, including the circumstances in which the evidence was obtained, the admission of the evidence would have such an adverse effect on the fairness of the proceedings that the court ought not to admit it.

The common law discretion applies where the court believes that the **prejudicial effect** of admitting a confession outweighs its **probative worth** (value in admitting it). The preservation of this discretion is set out in s 82(3) of the PACE Act 1984.

In contrast to the common law discretion the statutory power includes confessions, hearsay and any other classification of evidence. Breaches of the PACE Act 1984 COP, in this instance Codes C and E, are especially important here as they would be taken into account when the court is considering the exclusion of evidence under this provision (s 67(11) of the PACE Act 1984). The court has no inherent legal power to discipline the police but does have a duty to safeguard its own processes from an **abuse of process** and ensure fairness in its own proceedings. Section 78 may seem like a provision that runs counter to this but its intention was to promote compliance with procedures. You should note that a breach of the PACE Codes, unless serious and substantial, will not in itself preclude evidence from admission; counsel must still argue the point (see *R v Delaney* (1988) 88 Cr App R 338).

Section 78 has a prospective application and therefore only applies to prosecution evidence that has not yet been adduced and does not include the evidence a co-accused seeks to adduce. Where confessions are concerned, the court will normally act under the statutory power rather than the common law discretion. In *R v Mason* [1988] 1 WLR 139 the court held that the lies that the police told to both the accused and his lawyer had an adverse effect on the fairness of the proceedings.

Where agent provocateurs are concerned the evidence is unlikely to be excluded. In *R v Smurthwaite* [1994] 1 All ER 898 the Court of Appeal set down the guidelines on evidence obtained through an agent provocateur. The case concerned A looking for a contract killer to murder B. The court stated that the following should be considered when assessing whether the evidence has an adverse effect on the fairness of the proceedings:

- whether the accused was encouraged to commit an offence he or she would not have committed;

- the means that was used to entrap them;
- the role played by the agent in entrapping the accused; and
- the strength of the evidence.

An interesting discussion is currently raging as to the admissibility of confessions that are obtained through police intervention and the social media (Facebook, Google+, Twitter or YouTube). One lawyer has even suggested that the police may incite someone to confess to the commission of a crime by using a victim to make conversation via online messaging, for example Joan tweets Barry asking him why he did something. Barry's response could incriminate him, as we have seen with cases involving the London riots (*R v Blackshaw and Others* [2011] EWCA Crim 2312). The ECtHR has confirmed in *Texeira de Castro v Portugal* (1999) EHRR 101 that the public interest simply does not lie in using evidence that was obtained by reason of the police inciting someone to commit a crime.

EXCLUSION OF UNFAIR EVIDENCE – S 58 OF THE PACE ACT 1984

This provision states that an accused must be given access to legal advice. The right to access legal advice can be delayed where a serious arrestable offence has been committed but only if authorised by a senior officer or one with the rank of at least a Superintendent (s 58(8)). The delay of this right is seen as fairly serious action and therefore s 58(8) outlines the instances in which it may be done, these are:

> . . . where [the officer] has reasonable grounds for believing that the exercise of the right . . . at the time when the person detained desires to exercise it . . . will lead to interference with or harm to evidence connected with . . . an indictable offence . . . or interference with or physical injury to other persons . . . will lead to the alerting of other persons suspected of having committed such an offence but not yet arrested for it . . . or will hinder the recovery of any property obtained as a result of such an offence.

Section 58(8A) states that delay may be authorised where:

> . . . exercise of the right . . . at the time when the person detained desires to exercise it . . . will lead to the alerting of other persons suspected of having committed such an offence but not yet arrested for it or . . . will hinder the recovery of any property obtained as a result of such an offence. An officer may also authorise delay where he has reasonable grounds for believing that . . . the person detained for the indictable offence has benefited from his criminal conduct and the recovery of the value of the property constituting the benefit will be hindered by the exercise of the right.

Section 58(8B) adds '. . . for the purposes of subsection (8A) above the question whether a person has benefited from his criminal conduct is to be decided in accordance with Part 2 of the Proceeds of Crime Act 2002.'

The provisions require that the accused be informed of the delay and that the reason for the delay be recorded on the custody information sheets. Finally, where the reason for the delay no longer exists, no further delay may be authorised. The exercise of delay under these provisions has not been as exceptional as the courts would have hoped it would be (see *R v Samuel* [1988] 2 WLR 920).

EXCLUSION – THE EFFECT ON THE PROCEEDINGS

Where a confession is excluded then the party seeking to adduce it as evidence of guilt will not be able to do so. A co-accused may cross-examine the confessor on their statement to highlight something that may undermine the prosecution case against him or her.

On-the-spot questions

What are the risks associated with confession evidence?

To what extent can a court exclude evidence under s 78 of the PACE Act 1984?

Section 58 allows a court to delay an accused access to legal advice. Discuss the pros and cons of this action and any relevant safeguards.

SUMMARY

Confession evidence requires particular caution because of the risks that are associated with its admission. In addition this type of evidence is closely linked with the right to a fair trial under Article 6 of the ECHR. The PACE Act 1984 and the COP that accompany it outline the statutory scheme and practical rules that govern its admission, exclusion and use. The rules are designed to correct potential unfairness from arising.

FURTHER READING

Blair, J P, 'The roles of interrogation, perception, and individual differences in producing compliant false confessions.' *Psychology, Crime & Law*, 2007, 13(2), 173–186.
This article assesses the impact of interrogation tactics and perceptions that may lead to false confessions being made.

Landa, CS (2012). *Evidence: Question and Answers 2013–2014*, 10th edn. London: Routledge.
This textbook focuses on the application of the law of evidence with some interesting practical questions and guidance on answering assessment questions.

Taylor, LJ and Henderson, SE, 'Confessions: Consensus in idem?' (2002) SLT 40 325.
This article provides an overview of confessions from the perspective of forensic psychology and whether that can help adduce more reliable confessions.

Vaughan, K, 'Cross-examining on inadmissible confessions'. (1989) 86(40) Law Soc Gazette 23.
This is a case comment on *Lui Mei Lin v R* [1989] AC 288 (PC (HK)) and whether a defendant is entitled to cross-examine a co-defendant on a statement they made that was ruled inadmissible.

Web link:
You can find a copy of the most recently amended PACE Act 1984 COP at: www.gov.uk/police-and-criminal-evidence-act-1984-pace-codes-of-practice.

Chapter 9
Character evidence

LEARNING OUTCOMES

By the end of this chapter, you should be able to:

- Critically engage with the principles that relate to bad and good character evidence
- Understand why the Criminal Justice Act 2003 reformed the law on character evidence in criminal proceedings
- Evaluate the rules on the admission or exclusion of bad and good character evidence and its purpose and effect

---

INTRODUCTION

The discussion in this chapter focuses on character evidence, with an emphasis on criminal proceedings and the reforms brought around by the CJA 2003. This includes a brief look at what character evidence is for the purposes of the common law and statute, and the rules on the admission or exclusion of this evidence at trial. The discussion then shifts to the admission of character evidence in civil proceedings.

CHARACTER IN ENGLISH CRIMINAL LAW

There are two forms of character – good character and bad character – and a body of statutory and common law rules that accompanies both. The previous regime for admitting such evidence was described by the Law Commission in its report titled *Evidence of Bad Character in Criminal Proceedings Law Com No.273: 9 October 2001* and Sir Robin Auld's *Review of the criminal courts in England and Wales* (2001) as being haphazard and outdated. The discussion later in this chapter will reveal how they are defined and the evidential issues in proceedings, for instance where the credit or reliability of a witness or the accused's character may be in issue. It is important for you to realise that the general rule in English evidence law was that the prosecution was prohibited from adducing evidence of an accused's bad character, save in limited circumstances. This departed from the rule that relevant evidence is admissible but is a good example of how the court sought to protect the jury from evidence that was irrelevant to an accused's guilt but may have been given far more weight than it deserved. Further, the court keeps a watchful eye on any instances in which the **probative worth** of any particular piece of evidence is outweighed by the **prejudicial effect** it has.

The rationale that underpinned the tight control of this form of evidence is best served by an example. Damian is accused of murder; he has a range of previous offences recorded against him, which include instances of petty theft and criminal damage. The logic was as follows: if the jury knew that Damian had been convicted of committing other criminal offences then they may infer from that the fact that Damian has a predilection towards criminality. The fact that these previous offences are not ones that relate to violent conduct serves to highlight the potential risk.

Character and reputation – the common law

Iago in Shakespeare's *Othello* sums up the perception the English courts had of reputation as evidence of guilt. He stated, in response to Cassio's comment on losing his reputation that '. . . reputation is . . . [a] most false imposition' (act 2, scene 3). What Iago is saying is that reputation is a fictional quality on the basis upon which people make assumptions, inferences of judgements that can, in short, be wrong. Prior to the statutory regimes introduced by the CEA 1898 and the CJA 2003, evidence of good character was regulated by the common law and the normal method of adducing this was through character witnesses. Under the common law rules, the term 'character' referred to the witness's reputation and the evidence of an accused's good character was inadmissible where tendered to contradict prosecution evidence of guilt. However, evidence of reputation was admissible to show that an accused was less likely to have committed the offence because of his good deeds even though evidence of specific deeds was inadmissible. Reputation refers to the general estimation or regard in which the public hold someone. The character witness would confirm the general reputation of the accused and the prosecution could adduce evidence in rebuttal of the same (see *R v Rowton* (1865) Le & Ca 520 also known as the rule from *Rowton*). For example, if Madeline was accused of having committed an offence contrary to the law then a witness could be called to testify as to her 'general reputation': the witness could have said 'Madeline is an upstanding member of our community'. In rebuttal, a prosecution witness could be asked: 'What do you think of Madeline's general reputation?' The witness could reply, 'She is not an upstanding member of our community.' However, if that witness said 'Madeline is evil to the core and certainly no friend of mine,' this would have been inadmissible as evidence of Madeline's disposition rather than her general character. Thus, the evidence in rebuttal was also required to be related to general reputation; this was confirmed by the Court of Appeal in *R v Redgrave* (1982) 74 Cr App R 10. You should note that the current notion of bad character centre less on reputation and far more on the **previous antecedent history** (past convictions) of the accused.

On-the-spot question

Summarise the rule from *R v Rowton*.

Character under the Criminal Evidence Act 1898

For the first time in criminal proceedings a statute allowed the accused to testify as to his or her own disposition, rather than just evidence that related to an accused's reputation. For instance, Fernando could tell the court that he had done various good deeds, which resulted in a complex set of authorities being established. The Act raised a number of issues, for example s 1(2) stated that the accused could not be questioned on his bad character, but to confuse matters further this was subject to the exceptions outlined in Figure 9.1 (below).

In essence, the accused was protected by a shield that was only lost if one of these three subsections were satisfied. The accused and his or her lawyer were required to run their defence with a particular decorum. Section 1(2) of the CEA 1898 has been amended by the CJA 2003. The operation of this provision is now subject to s 101 of the CJA 2003 that now governs the admission of bad character evidence.

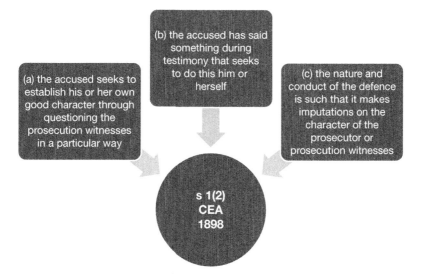

Figure 9.1 Questioning an accused on his or her bad character

In *R v Vye* [1993] 3 All ER 241 the court held that in a case where the accused has sought to establish his or her good character either during oral testimony in court or prior to this, for instance in a statement given to the police, then the trial judge should consider whether it would be appropriate to issue a two-point direction to the jury in terms of the use of that evidence by outlining:

(a) whether the accused is more likely to be telling the truth (the evidence is relevant to the accused's testimony in terms of credibility); and

(b) if the accused is likely to have committed the offence with which he or she is charged (the evidence is relevant to the accused's propensity to commit the offence).

A *Vye* direction focused the attention of the jury to the accused's good character, which would have a positive effect on them. You should note that a direction, tailored to the circumstances of the case, could be given where good character evidence was adduced regardless of whether the statements seeking to establish it were at trial or prior to it. Furthermore, the accused did not have to testify at trial in his or her own defence in order for a direction to be given – think back to the rules on competence and compellability and the fact that an accused cannot be compelled to give evidence on his or her own behalf, even though they are competent (CEA 1898). Nor, subject to the later discussion, could the accused be cross-examined on his or her previous bad character by reason of privilege (see Chapter 5). The trial judge would also consider the appropriateness of a direction where an accused with good character was jointly tried with someone of bad character. This law was approved by the House of Lords in *R v Aziz* [1995] 3 All ER 149 with the added point that the role of the trial judge was also to ensure that the jury received a balanced and fair picture of the entire case.

On-the-spot question

 What purpose does a Vye direction serve?

Bad character under the common law as similar fact evidence

The doctrine of similar fact evidence was abolished by the CJA 2003; it provided that evidence of an accused's disposition was admissible where it was similar to the offence with which they stood charged, for example evidence of Samira's previous conduct that related to acts of violence where she stood charged with assault occasioning an actual bodily harm contrary to the Offences against the Persons Act 1864. Similar fact evidence was evidence that showed an accused to have propensity towards the commission of particular types of offences. It was prejudicial in that it was a negative presentation of the accused, an issue that highlights the inherent weaknesses in human nature in terms of persuasion.

In *Makin v AG for New South Wales* [1894] AC 57 the court outlined the test for the admission of similar fact evidence: where evidence is relevant to a matter before the jury bearing on the issue as to whether the accused committed the crime. In this case, the Makins stood accused of murdering a child whose remains were found buried in their garden. The court gave permission to the prosecution that allowed it to adduce evidence showing that the remains of other missing children had been found in each of the homes that the couple had occupied over a period of years.

You should note that this form of evidence would only be admissible where the court was satisfied that any prejudicial effect was outweighed by its probative worth (relevance and persuasion). Further, such evidence was required to be supported by an appropriate warning from the trial judge (see *Boardman v DPP* [1975] AC 421).

The law relating to similar fact evidence was abolished by ss 101(1)(c) and (d) and s 101(3) of the CJA 2003, however the court's decision in *R v Hanson* highlighted that the previous case law would continue to apply to the new provisions. These are discussed later but you should note that where the evidence would have an adverse effect on the fairness of the proceedings then the court is unlikely to admit it. This will be especially true of offences that were committed many years ago.

Current law in criminal proceedings

The CJA 2003 introduced a fundamental change to this area of evidence law; it provides that bad character evidence that is relevant to a case is admissible. The statute abolished the general rule that excluded the admission of evidence of misconduct and bad character. The 2003 Act laid down the circumstances in which such evidence would be admissible. Prior to its enactment questions arose as to the legality of such a step in terms of the right to a fair trial guaranteed by Article 6 of the ECHR. The European decisions in *X v Austria, Yearbook VII* (1965) 481 1855/63 and *Unterpertinger v Austria* [1991] 13 EHRR 175 confirm that the admission of previous convictions that relate to the matters of a case do not breach the right to a fair trial. The reasoning that supported these findings was the fact that the practice of admitting bad character evidence varied across the European Union member states, of which the United Kingdom is a member.

The changes made by the CJA 2003 in relation to the admission of bad character evidence do not have the effect of placing a greater burden on the accused to prove his or her innocence; this would in effect be akin to imposing a reverse burden of proof on the accused (see Chapter 2). They do however make it easier for the prosecution to discharge the legal burden in proving that the defendant is guilty of committing the crime (see *R v Cowan* [1996] QB 373). The statutory scheme revolves around minimising the risk from the consideration of irrelevant previous convictions. The admission of such evidence should be a judgement call for the prosecution, taking into account the case at hand and the facts of the previous conviction itself by looking for shared special features, continued propensity or the accused's entire criminal record (*R v Hanson, R v Gilmore, R v Pickstone* [2005] EWCA Crim 824).

It was clear from the enactment of the CJA 2003 that parliament intended for bad character evidence to be put before the court on a more regular basis. The first enquiry of the court will normally be whether to use the gateways for the admission of such evidence at all (see *R v Edwards (Stewart Dean)* [2005] EWCA Crim 3244). Questions of the weight to be attributed to this evidence are a matter for the jury but subject to (a) the trial judge's powers under s 107 (stopping a case where the evidence is contaminated, for instance fabricated or concocted), (b) directions the trial judge may wish to issue in terms of relevance and (c) any other matters (see *R v Hanson (Nicky)* [2005] EWCA Crim 824 and *R v Highton (Edward Paul)* [2005] EWCA Crim 1985).

You should note that the provisions apply for the admission of bad character evidence of an accused and of witnesses, the latter for purposes of discrediting them. Figure 9.2 summarises the provisions that will be considered in this chapter:

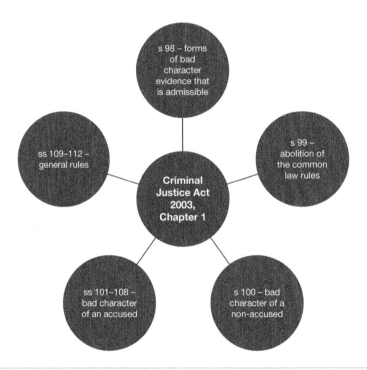

Figure 9.2 Bad character and the CJA 2003

Section 98 of the CJA 2003 – defining bad character

Sections 98(a) and (b) of the CJA 2003 define bad character as

> . . . evidence of . . . or of a disposition towards, misconduct on his part, other than evidence which . . . has to do with the alleged facts of the offence with which the defendant is charged, or is evidence of misconduct in connection with the investigation or prosecution of that offence.

This applies to both the accused and any witnesses that are party to the proceedings. The most salient parts are 'disposition towards' or 'misconduct on his [or her] part', which, incidentally, can be anything that occurs before or after the matter that is being tried. Such evidence includes any acquittals, convictions, stays in proceedings (*R v Edwards* [2006] 1 WLR 1524) and the facts that surround those. You should note that the courts are wary in admitting evidence of previous acquittals because they may lead the jury to infer that even though the accused was acquitted he or she was probably guilty (*R v Harrison* [2004] EWCA Crim 1792).

The provision also provides two exclusions: bad character evidence does not include evidence that '. . . has to do with the alleged facts of the offence with which the defendant is charged' or '. . . evidence of misconduct in connection with the investigation or prosecution of that offence'. Where either of these exceptions applies the test is one of relevance. The question will be whether this evidence (a) relates to a fact in issue and (b) whether it proves any element of the offence charged. Therefore, evidence that relates to either of these exceptions is subject to the normal rules of evidence law (see *R v Edwards* [2006] 3 All ER 882). This may be evidence that Dorothy criminally damaged Stan's car while shouting obscenities at him. She also tried to resist arrest by trying to escape from PC Patrillo, who arrived at the scene after a frantic call from Stan. All the facts are relevant: the former in relation to the commission of the offence of criminal damage and possibly assault (exception one), and resisting arrest by trying to escape (exception two); these do not amount to bad character evidence and will be admitted as evidence of guilt. In *R v Malone* [2006] All ER (D) 321 the court allowed the prosecution to adduce a forged document to prove that A and B were in dispute with one another. In essence, the effect of the two exceptions is to admit evidence that will prejudice the accused outside of (a) the common law rules on reputation preserved by s 99 and (b) the statutory scheme for admission provided by ss 100 and 101 (discussed below).

On-the-spot question

Why do you think that parliament did not define misconduct to include 'evidence to do with the alleged facts of the offence with which the defendant is charged' or 'evidence of misconduct in connection with the investigation or prosecution of that offence'?

Section 99 of the CJA 2003 – abolition of the common law rules

Section 99 of the Act provides that

> . . . the common law rules governing the admissibility of evidence of bad
> character in criminal proceedings are abolished . . . [this is] subject to Section
> 118(1) in so far as it preserves the rule under which, in criminal proceedings, a
> person's reputation is admissible for the purposes of proving his bad character.

This has the effect of (a) abolishing the common law rules and (b) preserving the rules
under which evidence of reputation is admissible, which includes:

- public information (records, published works and public documents);
- reputation as to character whether good or bad (s 118(2));
- reputation as to family tradition (s 118(3));
- res gestae (s 118(4));
- confessions (s 118(5));
- admissions (s 118(6)); and
- expert evidence (s 118(8)).

On-the-spot question

Why were the common law rules abolished and some of them replaced by
statutory provisions?

Sections 100 and 101 of the CJA 2003 – the statutory scheme for the admission of bad character evidence of a non-accused and the accused

Section 100(1) of the CJA 2003 sets out the instances in which bad character evidence of
someone other than the accused can be adduced in a criminal trial. It provides that:

> . . . in criminal proceedings evidence of the bad character of a person other than
> the defendant is [only] admissible if . . . (a) it is important explanatory evidence,
> (b) it has substantial probative value in relation to a matter which . . . is a matter
> in issue in the proceedings, and . . . is of substantial importance in the context
> of the case as a whole . . . or (c) all parties to the proceedings agree to the
> evidence being admissible.

The provision has the effect of making the admission of witness or non-witnesses bad character evidence more restrictive than under the common law.

Section 100(2) outlines that important explanatory evidence is evidence, without which the court or jury would find it difficult or impossible to understand the other evidence before them and evidence that has a substantial value in helping them understand the case as a whole. Under s 100(3) when assessing probative value under s 100(1)(b) the court will take into account various factors as summarised in Figure 9.3 (below).

The instances in which bad character evidence is admissible as evidence against an accused in criminal proceedings is outlined in s 101 of the CJA 2003, which provides that:

> . . . evidence of the defendant's bad character is admissible [only if] (a) all parties to the proceedings agree to the evidence being admissible, (b) the evidence is adduced by the defendant himself or is given in answer to a question asked by him in cross-examination and intended to elicit it, (c) it is important explanatory evidence, (d) it is relevant to an important matter in issue between the defendant and the prosecution, (e) it has substantial probative value in relation

Figure 9.3 Section 100(3) considerations for the admission of evidence under s 100(1)(b)

to an important matter in issue between the defendant and a co-defendant, (f) it is evidence to correct a false impression given by the defendant, or (g) the defendant has made an attack on another person's character.

On-the-spot question

 Summarise what is meant by the term important explanatory evidence.

KEY CASE ANALYSIS: *R v O'Leary (Patrick)* [2013] EWCA Crim 1371

Background

The accused, a self-employed roofer, was convicted of making false representations to two pensioners, contrary to the Fraud Act 2006, and two counts of theft. Victim one was an old lady who had dementia; the accused had not actually done the roofing work he was employed to do but had charged the victim £200. The second was an elderly man who also suffered from dementia and had paid O'Leary £5,000 (two cheques, each valued at £2,500) to do some work. The trial judge allowed the prosecution to adduce evidence of his previous conviction for the burglary of a 92-year-old pensioner's home and that all the evidence was cross-admissible. The evidence was designed to show that he had a propensity towards choosing pensioners as his victims. This resulted in the accused being convicted and sentenced to a total of six years' imprisonment.

Principle established

The court, in dismissing O'Leary's appeal, stated that evidence of the previous conviction and the cross-admissibility of the facts was relied on to show that the accused preyed on the vulnerable. Further it was not unfairly prejudicial evidence under s 78 of the PACE Act 1984 because the accused had told the jury that he had a clean record (no convictions), a lie that the prosecution was entitled to rebut.

Section 112(1) of the CJA 2003 defines 'misconduct' as the '. . . commission of an offence or other reprehensible behaviour'. The latter is not defined, which has left a broad scope for interpretation, and it is commonly suggested that disciplinary action, omissions or behaviour regarded as wrong by a particular sect of society may fall within this (see *R v Osbourne* [2007] EWCA Crim 481). Section 109 provides that a '. . . reference to the relevance or probative value of evidence is a reference to relevance or probative value on the assumption that it is true.' The latter is qualified by s 109(2) that states that a court may decide that the evidence is not true because no reasonable tribunal could come to that judgement on the basis of any other material that is before it. For instance, Magda stands charged with the commission of five assaults. At each trial she alleges that the victim approached her first and that she was merely acting in self-defence. She is acquitted of four of those charges. At the trial for the fifth the prosecution calls the other four victims to testify and negate her defence. It is likely that this evidence will be adduced under these provisions on the basis of s 101(c) or (d) as important explanatory evidence or it is relevant to an important matter in issue (see *R v West* [2003] EWCA Crim 3024). Additionally, an allegation of assault made by Magda against Fanny, which she subsequently drops is unlikely to have enough probative worth to be admissible under s 101(e) (see *R v Bovell* [2005] 2 Cr App R 401). What follows is a brief discussion of each of the gateways.

Gateway one s 101(1)(a) – all parties to the proceedings agree to the evidence being admissible

This provision allows for the admission of an accused's previous convictions where the parties agree to their admission. This is likely to be unusual; tactically the accused would probably want this evidence to be withheld because of the impact it is likely to have in terms of propensity or to show that the accused had a particular predilection, as in *O'Leary* (above). Unless of course this evidence may come up at trial in due course, in which case tendering it may receive some credit from the jury. In any regard it has to be (a) relevant and (b) the trial judge still has to permit its admission.

Gateway two s 101(1)(b) – the evidence is adduced by the defendant himself or is given in answer to a question asked by him in cross-examination and intended to elicit it

There are a number of parts to this section. First, evidence of bad character can be adduced by the accused him- or herself; once again this will be unusual. However, an application under this provision cannot be refused by the trial judge (see *R v Edwards (Stewart Dean)* [2005] EWCA Crim 3244), once again subject to the trial judge's discretion under s 107 (contaminated evidence). The accused may state that he or she has been 'in trouble' on a previous occasion as in *Jones v DPP* [1962] AC 635. Second the accused may ask a co-accused or a prosecution witness a question intending to elicit this evidence. The point is that it is the accused who must either adduce the evidence or intend for it to be adduced through his or her lawyer's questioning. The provision has caused a few issues in terms of its clarity, for example if Hilary stands charged of murder and she calls Julie as a witness in her defence, where (a) Hilary asks Julie, 'You know about my troubled past' and (b) Julie makes this unsolicited comment 'You have changed after all that trouble with the police when you were younger.' – the former clearly falls under s 101(1)(b) and the latter outside of it.

Gateway three s 101(1)(c) – it is important explanatory evidence

Section 101(2) defines important explanatory evidence for the purposes of this provision as '[Evidence] without [which] . . . the court or jury would find it impossible or difficult properly to understand other evidence in the case, and . . . its value for understanding the case as a whole is substantial.'

The concept is similar to the now abolished common law rules on evidence that lends background and context. In *R v West* [2003] EWCA Crim 3024 the court allowed the prosecution to adduce evidence of lengthy sexual grooming that had led to the sexual abuse for which the accused was being tried. Important explanatory evidence may also include a previous acquittal, but the court would have to judge this on its merits and in accordance with its discretion to exclude on the basis of ss 78 and 82 of the PACE Act 1984. A previous acquittal will be relevant evidence for an offence with which the accused currently stands charged but which also amounts to evidence of guilt in relation to an offence for which the accused is no longer indicted. Such evidence may be adduced to prove that the accused knows of a particular fact where the accused denies this. You should note that the old authorities on the admission of background evidence have varied in their approach.

Gateway four s 101(1)(d) – it is relevant to an important matter in issue between the defendant and the prosecution

This provision allows the prosecution to adduce evidence of an accused's 'propensity' to commit crimes or be untruthful, which relates to a matter in issue that is of substantial importance in the context of the whole case. There are two forms of evidential relevance that you should be aware of: (a) evidence relevant to a matter in issue and (b) evidence relevant to credibility. This provision focuses on the former unless the credibility of the accused is itself a matter in issue then evidence relating to his or her bad character may help determine it – this is akin to, but far broader than, the common law concept of similar fact evidence. The term 'matter in issue' is defined by ss 103(1)(a) – (b), what offences show propensity is outlined in ss 103(2)(a) – (b) and ss 103(4)(a) – (b). In short the result is that evidence adduced under this gateway shows one of two things:

- the accused has a propensity to commit the type of crime that is of the same description or category with which he or she is charged and therefore is likely to have committed this one (the latter is the implication); or

- the accused has a propensity to be untruthful and that therefore he or she cannot be believed.

For instance, Wilhelm takes what he believes to be a genuine Picasso painting to sell to an art dealer. The dealer confirms that the painting is in fact a very poor forgery. Wilhelm then takes the same painting to two other art dealers, with the knowledge that the painting is a fake, and tries to pass it off as a genuine painting, both of whom tell him that the painting is a fake. He finally manages to sell it to a novice art dealer who relies on his representations. Evidence of his lies to the second and third art dealers may be admissible under this gateway to prove the fact that he knew (a) the painting was a forgery and (b) its true value (see *R v Francis* (1874) LR 2 CCR 278). Where the credibility of the accused is itself a matter in issue then evidence relating to the bad character of an accused may help determine it – this is akin to but far broader than the common law concept of similar fact evidence (see also *R v J* [2013] EWCA Crim 1050 and *R v Cambridge (Connor)* [2011] EWCA Crim 2009). You should note that the statute does not define what amounts to a crime of the same 'description' or 'category'; the words however speak for themselves. In deciding whether to admit this evidence the trial judge will normally ask him or herself two questions: does this evidence make it more likely that the accused committed the offence (propensity) and is it unfair or unjust to allow the evidence to go before the court. In terms of the latter the court will take into account the length of time that has elapsed between the explanatory evidence and the current charge (s 103(3) of the CJA 2003).

On-the-spot question

 What is the purpose of adducing evidence that relates to propensity?

Gateway five s 101(1)(e) – it has substantial probative value in relation to an important matter in issue between the defendant and a co-defendant

Under this gateway an accused will only be allowed to adduce evidence of a co-accused's bad character if it relates to an important matter in issue between them. Additionally, the evidence must have substantial probative value in that regard. Therefore, if Akira and Lucy are charged with the murder of Fran and they both state that the other committed the crime, then Akira may wish to adduce evidence that Lucy has a violent disposition and is more likely to have killed Fran then her (see *R v Randall* [2003] 2 Cr App R 442). In *R v Phillips (Paul Edward)* [2012] Lloyd's Rep F C 179 the accused appealed following conviction on the basis that the trial judge had wrongly excluded bad character evidence of a co-accused that had substantial probative value. The court held that even though this was the case the conviction was still safe.

Gateway six s 101(1)(f) – it is evidence to correct a false impression given by the defendant

This gateway will apply where an accused has, either expressly or by implication, given the jury a false impression about his or her character. In that instance the prosecution may adduce evidence of bad character in response so that the view the jury forms on the basis of the evidence is a corrected one. For example at Chanelle's trial for Graham's murder she states, 'I've always been a quiet person and kept myself to myself.' If she has a series of previous convictions for violence, theft and criminal damage then such a comment would open up the possibility for the prosecution to adduce evidence to correct the image Chanelle has portrayed of herself.

Section 105(1)(a) provides that:

> . . . the defendant gives a false impression if he is responsible for the making of an express or implied assertion which is apt to give the court or jury a false or misleading impression about [themselves] . . . (b) evidence to correct such an impression is evidence which has probative value in correcting it.

Further under s 105(2) an accused:

> . . . is treated as being responsible for the making of an assertion if . . . the assertion is made by the defendant in the proceedings (whether or not in evidence given by him), the assertion was made by the defendant on being questioned under caution, before charge, about the offence with which he is charged, or on being charged with the offence or officially informed that he might be prosecuted for it, and evidence of the assertion is given in the proceedings, the assertion is made by a witness called by the defendant, the assertion is made by any witness in cross-examination in response to a question asked by the defendant that is intended to elicit it, or is likely to do so, or the assertion was made by any person out of court, and the defendant adduces evidence of it in the proceedings.

Gateway seven s 101(1)(g) – the defendant has made an attack on another person's character

This provision allows evidence of an accused's bad character to be adduced where he or she makes an attack on the character of the prosecution or its witnesses, the victim, the police or anyone else, whether they are alive or dead. This is similar to the old rules under the CEA 1898 and the rationale here is that the accused should not be allowed to undermine the credibility of another person and protect his or her own true character. The instances in which an attack will be considered to have been made are outlined in s 106(1) of the CJA 2003, as follows:

KEY CASE ANALYSIS: *R v B (Richard William)* [2008] EWCA Crim 1850

Background

The accused stood charged with the rape of his 13-year-old daughter and sexual assault of his stepson aged 8. The latter occurred two years after the alleged rape. The prosecution was allowed to adduce evidence that the accused had had sexual activity with his 9-year-old nephew when he was aged 14 to show he had a propensity to commit the types of offences with which he was now charged. He was convicted and he appealed on the basis that (a) this evidence should not have been admitted, (b) the count of rape did not form the part of a series of offences that were the same or of a similar character to the counts of sexual activity with a child because there were distinct differences in terms of the gender of the victims and the gaps of time between the offences, therefore they should have appeared on separate indictments. Further, that his conviction for raping a 16-year-old girl should not have been admitted as evidence of propensity because of the difference in the age of the victims (14 and 16); neither should evidence of the fact that he had shown his niece a book on sex positions where it was used to correct a false impression given by him at interview.

Principle established

The court allowed the appeal on the basis that (a) the evidence should not have been admitted even though it was evidence of his propensity for homosexual conduct as it had an adverse effect on the fairness of the proceedings under the CJA 2003 s 101(3). The court also stated **obiter** that the time between the commission of offences will not prevent them from forming a part of a series of similar offences provided they were closely related. Here the offences had been correctly joined on the same indictment as in *Ludlow v Metropolitan Police Commissioner* [1971] A.C. 29 and *R v Baird (Paul)* (1993) 97 Cr App R 308. The previous conviction of rape was admissible as it contained similarities with the current offences, for instance that they were committed in a car. Finally, that the accused's negative response to the question, 'Are you interested in young girls?' while being interviewed did create a false impression that needed correcting under s 101(1)(f).

Where the accused disassociates him- or herself from the assertion then they will not be taken as having made it (s 105(3)). Finally, the court may treat the accused as having given a false impression of its own accord but it must assess whether the conduct of the accused is apt to give that misleading impression.

- the accused adduces any evidence that attacks the character of the other person;
- the accused or his or her representative asks a question in cross-examination that is intended to elicit such evidence or is likely to do so;
- evidence of an imputation about the other person made by the accused under caution, before charge, about the offence with which they are charged, on being charged or officially informed that they might be prosecuted for that offence, is given in evidence.

Therefore the accused should be careful as to the words they use, for instance colloquialisms or flippant comments such as 'he's as bent as the rest of the coppers' and anything they say in the heat of the moment such as 'she started it, she always does and she's been to jail for offences relating to violence' will all fall under this gateway.

Section 106(2) states that evidence attacking the other person's character means '. . . evidence to the effect that the other person . . . has committed an offence (whether a different offence from the one with which the defendant is charged or the same one), or has behaved, or is disposed to behave, in a reprehensible way.' The vital question is what amounts to 'reprehensible way'.

On-the-spot question

What is the rationale that underpins adducing an accused's bad character under s 101(1)(g)?

KEY CASE ANALYSIS: *R v C* [2011] EWCA Crim 939

Background

The accused stood charged with having committed sexual offences against two children. The accused made an allegation that the older child had made up the entire allegations to get back at him and had put the younger child up to making them too. This resulted in the prosecution being allowed under s 101(1)(g) to adduce the accused's previous convictions for various offences dating back to 1977 (including robbery, actual bodily harm and firearms offences). The accused was convicted and appealed.

Principle established

The court held in line with *R v Jenkins* (1945) 31 Cr App R 1 at page 15 that it was fair where an accused attacked the credibility of a witness that material be put before the jury that allowed them to judge the accused and whether or not he or she was worthy of belief (approved in *Selvey v DPP* [1970] AC 304).

Therefore, all convictions are potentially relevant under gateway (g) as general rather than detailed assistance to the jury in judging the character of the accused. Basically, the trial judge may admit evidence that may damage the accused's character so that the jury are able to assess the merits of each version of the facts with which they are presented. You should note that only the prosecution may adduce evidence under this provision (see s 106(3)).

CHARACTER IN CIVIL PROCEEDINGS

Civil courts were reticent to accept evidence of a criminal conviction as evidence in civil proceedings; the rationale that underpinned this related to the risk of prejudice that would be created – it was thought that the knowledge of a finding made in a criminal court on a matter may influence the finding that a civil court would make. The logic was flawed because very little is achieved where a civil court is required to go through the same process in relation to a particular point, especially because the standard of proof is lower than that of the criminal courts. To avoid a risk of the court's decision being influenced, a criminal conviction can only be used as evidence in specified matters as outlined in s 7 of the CEA 1995 and ss 11–13 of the CEA 1968. These provisions allow evidence relating to the defendant's reputation, previous criminal convictions and findings made in relation to adultery (discussed below) to be adduced in a civil trial.

Criminal convictions

Section 11(1) of the CEA 1968 provides:

> . . . in any civil proceedings the fact that a person has been convicted of an offence by or before any court in the United Kingdom . . . shall be admissible in evidence for the purpose of proving, where to do so is relevant to any issue in those proceedings, that he committed that offence, whether he was so convicted upon a plea of guilty or otherwise and whether or not he is a party to the civil proceedings; but no conviction other than a subsisting one shall be admissible in evidence by virtue of this section.

This provision requires that the criminal conviction must be one by a court of the United Kingdom and that there must be no appeal of the criminal conviction pending. Where a party challenges the criminal conviction then they must prove that it is not relevant or non-existent (see *Taylor v Taylor* [1970] 1 WLR 1148).

Section 11(2) supports s 11(1) and provides that:

> . . . in any civil proceedings in which by virtue of this section a person is proved to have been convicted of an offence . . . he shall be taken to have committed

that offence unless the contrary is proved; and . . . for the purpose of identifying the facts on which the conviction was based, the contents of any document which is admissible as evidence of the conviction . . . the contents of the information, complaint, indictment or charge-sheet . . . shall be admissible in evidence for that purpose.

This means that the court presumes the person to have committed the offence unless that person proves the contrary.

Under these provisions the party seeking to rely on the previous criminal conviction must state that they will do so from the outset.

On-the-spot question

 Why do you think the approach to the admission of bad character evidence varied between the civil and criminal courts?

Matrimonial proceedings: a finding of adultery or paternity

Section 12(1) of the CEA 1968 states that:

. . . in any civil proceedings . . . the fact that a person has been found guilty of adultery in any matrimonial proceedings . . . and the fact that a person has been found to be the father of a child in relevant proceedings before any court in England and Wales shall be admissible in evidence for the purpose of proving, where to do so is relevant to any issue in those civil proceedings, that he committed the adultery to which the finding relates or . . . [he] is (or was) the father of that child, whether or not he offered any defence to the allegation of adultery or paternity and whether or not he is a party to the civil proceedings; but no finding or adjudication other than a subsisting one shall be admissible in evidence by virtue of this section.

Again this requires the finding to have been made by a court in England and Wales. Section 12(2) provides that:

. . . in any civil proceedings . . . in which . . . a person is proved to have been found guilty of adultery as mentioned or . . . to have been found or adjudged to be the father of a child as mentioned . . . he shall be taken to have committed the adultery to which the finding relates or, as the case may be, to be (or have been) the father of that child, unless the contrary is proved . . . and without prejudice to the reception of any other admissible evidence for the purpose of identifying the facts on which the finding or adjudication was based, the contents of any document which was before the court, or which contains any pronouncement of the court, in the other proceedings . . . in question shall be admissible in evidence for that purpose.

This means that the court presumes the person to have been adulterous or accepts that a finding of paternity is made out unless that person proves the contrary.

Again, under these provisions the party that seeks to rely on the findings must state that they will do so from the outset.

Conclusiveness of convictions for cases of defamation

Section 13(1) of the CEA 1968 states that:

. . . in an action for libel or slander in which the question whether the plaintiff did or did not commit a criminal offence is relevant to an issue arising in the action, proof that, at the time when that issue falls to be determined . . . he stands convicted of that offence shall be conclusive evidence that he committed that offence; and his conviction thereof shall be admissible in evidence accordingly.

Section 13(2) provides that:

. . . in any such action as aforesaid in which by virtue of this section the plaintiff is proved to have been convicted of an offence, the contents of any document which is admissible as evidence of the conviction, and the contents of the information, complaint, indictment or charge-sheet on which . . . he was convicted, shall, without prejudice to the reception of any other admissible evidence for the purpose of identifying the facts on which the conviction was based, be admissible in evidence for the purpose of identifying those facts.

These final two provisions allow a criminal conviction for libel or slander to be conclusive evidence that the person convicted committed the offence. Where the presumption applies in relation to a witness it can be rebutted (see s 12 of the Defamation Act 1996).

Similar fact evidence

In civil cases the parties to the action can also adduce evidence of previous misconduct as similar fact evidence that leads to an inference (**circumstantial evidence**) that helps prove a fact in issue. To be admitted this evidence has to be (a) probative, (b) the facts must be similar to those before the court and (c) the court should consider whether it should admit it taking into account all the circumstances (see *O'Brien v Chief Constable of South Wales Police* [2005] UKHL 26 and *DPP v P* [1991] 2 AC 447). Where the evidence is probative there is no requirement for inexplicable similarity before the evidence can be admitted in civil proceedings, however any level of similarity will most likely make the evidence easier to admit. When assessing whether to admit such evidence the court will take into account factors similar to, but not the same as, those in criminal proceedings. The court will carry out a balancing exercise and will for that purpose consider unfairness or hardship but not the level of prejudice that will be suffered by the defendant if it were admitted, how the evidence was obtained and the level of its probative value. In *Hales v Kerr* [1908] 2 KB 601, in an action for professional negligence, the court permitted the evidence of two witnesses who confirmed that they too had contracted an infection from the same barber's shop. The evidence was relevant because it showed by inference that on the **balance of probabilities** (a) the cutting implements were not disinfected and therefore (b) the barber fell short of the standard required of a professional person, namely he had been negligent.

The court has the discretion to exclude evidence should it find that its processes are being abused (**abuse of process**), where it believes that such evidence was obtained in a manner that is contrary to the law of the land or the spirit of the Civil Procedure Rules 2013.

SUMMARY

Until the introduction of the CJA 2003 character evidence was regarded as being highly prejudicial because of assumptions it led to and its impact on the jury. The changes brought around by the 2003 statute has meant that the use of this form of evidence has become commonplace in the criminal courts. One thing is certain; the Act has broadened the definition and circumstances in which this character evidence is admissible while simultaneously restricting its use by the defence in relation to witnesses and non-witnesses. Character in criminal proceedings includes previous antecedents and misconduct. In civil proceedings, similar fact evidence has been routinely admitted.

FURTHER READING

Landa, CS (2012). *Evidence: Question and Answers 2013–2014*, 10th edn. London: Routledge.
This textbook focuses on the application of the law of evidence with some interesting practical questions and guidance on answering assessment questions.

Munday, R, 'What constitutes "other reprehensible behaviour" under the bad character provisions of the CJA 2003?' [2005] Jan Crim LR 24.
This article investigates the reconfiguration and redefinition of the rules that govern the admission of bad character evidence in criminal proceedings.

Tain, P, 'Bad character' (2004) SLJ 148(48) 1449.
This article focuses on the admissibility of bad character evidence in relation to a non-accused as well as the accused and the duty of the court in excluding evidence that would affect the fairness of the proceedings.

Wilcock, P and Bennathan, J, 'The new meaning of bad character' (2004) 154(7136) NLJ 1054.
This article explores character evidence under the CJA 2003 including its contamination.

Chapter 10
Documentary, real, expert and opinion evidence

LEARNING OUTCOMES

By the end of this chapter, you should be able to:

* Critically engage with the principles that relate to opinion evidence
* Understand and evaluate the rules on the admission or exclusion of expert and opinion evidence and its purpose and effect
* Determine who the law considers to be an expert
* Engage with the rules on documentary and real evidence

INTRODUCTION

The discussion in this chapter focuses on opinion documentary, opinion and real evidence. The discussion begins with a look at documentary and real evidence and then shifts to opinion evidence. The latter includes a brief look at who is an expert for the purposes of the law and the nature and purpose of this form of evidence at trial.

DOCUMENTARY EVIDENCE

The English law of evidence is a set of rules and exceptions that comes together to aid the judge and jury to mentally recreate what may have happened within a given situation. Documentary can be best (or primary) evidence; this is considered to be the most reliable type of proof that is available. Therefore, greater confidence is lent to an original document albeit that a certified copy (secondary evidence) is often acceptable. An original document is proof of primary facts; assumed facts (secondary facts) can only be assumed if they can properly lead to that conclusion (see Chapter 1).

Documentary evidence comes in a number of forms, for instance it may amount to hearsay if it is tendered to prove the truth of its contents, non-hearsay where it is tendered to show that it merely exists or is a confession statement (see Chapter 8). Documentary evidence may also be classed as direct evidence, such as a lease or tenancy agreement or as an aid to recall events or facts that are now in the past, for example in court by a witness looking to refresh his or her memory (see Chapter 4). Therefore documents, as evidence, must satisfy the requirements for relevance and admissibility. Documents can be defined as electronic (including fax, email and telex), photographic or written matter that provide information or act as official records.

Sometimes certified copies of documents can amount to best evidence, for instance if John is required to lodge an original with a bank or other institution then a certified copy of that document will be accepted as best evidence. An example of such a document was a set of property title deeds where the property was purchased with a mortgage – before the digitalisation of the land registry the bank used to retain these. For the purposes of civil proceedings documents are defined to include audio recordings – whether analogue or digital – photographs, or soundtracks and video films, for example CCTV footage (s 10(1) of the Civil Evidence Act 1968). The common law, the PACE Act 1984 and the CJA 2003 and any common law rule preserved by it now govern the admission of documentary hearsay evidence in criminal proceedings. Under the common law the person seeking to rely on a document must produce an original or certified copy of a document in court. You should note that the latter was not previously acceptable because of the risk of fabrication, an issue that has been resolved by sophisticated modern techniques and the creation of new forms of documents (see *Kajala v Noble* (1982) 75 Cr App R 149).

Only rarely will secondary evidence be admitted in lieu of primary or best evidence. This form of evidence includes copies of original documents that have been destroyed, lost or the relevant part of a banker's book. It may be that the holder of the original document who is not party to the proceedings has refused to allow the party seeking it rely on it to 'borrow' it for that purpose. Figure 10.1 summarises the position:

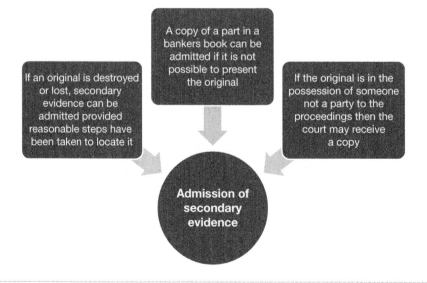

Figure 10.1 Admission of secondary evidence as best evidence

On-the-spot question

What do you think is the rationale for the admission of best evidence?

REAL EVIDENCE

Real evidence is tangible evidence that is observed or inspected in court, allowing the jury to draw inferences (conclusions) from it. A machete that had been used to murder someone would be an example of this type of evidence, or items such as photographs of a crime scene or a victim or witness; these categories are not mutually exclusive. Real evidence must be authentic and of good quality but may be circumstantial, for example crime stains that are used to extract DNA evidence (*R v Stevenson* [1971] 1 WLR 1). The point to note is that real evidence must be something that makes an impression on the court.

OPINION EVIDENCE

The evidence of a witness should be based purely on the events that they have personally perceived. They should avoid speculation, making assumptions, drawing conclusions or giving their own opinion because of the risks attached. For example it would be inappropriate if Alice, who is not an expert in physiognomy (reading the characteristics in faces), gave her opinion in relation to the identity of an assailant on the basis of a blurred image from some dated CCTV footage. The jury are at risk of attributing too much weight to such speculative evidence that has little probative worth (lacks the quality to prove something). Generally, the English law of evidence excludes the opinion evidence of witnesses. The only permissible forms of opinion are as follows:

* expert evidence;
* eyewitness opinion; and
* opinion of an accused's general reputation.

Expert opinion evidence

There are matters that the court will judicially note in accordance with its own competence and experience. However, where a court encounters an issue that is beyond its competence and experience, for instance medical or scientific evidence relating to the likely causes of the death of unborn babies, foreign law, trade practices or the identification of an assailant using facial mapping, then it may call an expert to assist it. In *Folkes v Chadd* (1782) 3 Doug KB 157 the court summarised the requirements before expert evidence could be adduced. It stated that first the evidence of an expert will be beyond the competence, experience and expertise of a normal person and therefore he or she can form an opinion on the basis of their expertise. You should note that educational qualifications in themselves do not denote who amounts to an expert. Therefore, someone with years of experience in dealing with a particular field may satisfy the second requirement that the expert be 'qualified'. Further, in civil proceedings, the evidence of a non-expert witness that conveys an opinion of the facts as they perceived them to be is admissible, for example 'Sharon was drunk, she was clutching a bottle of Jack Daniels and was stumbling all over the place' (see s 3(2) of the Civil Evidence Act 1972). Other facts that may fall under this include an eyewitness identification, the speed of a car and the value of a particular item, for instance an iPad costs roughly around £300.

The main difference between expert evidence in civil and criminal proceedings is that in the latter the expert is eligible to give evidence on any relevant matter, including those that are facts in issue (s 3 of the Civil Evidence Act 1972). Furthermore, in civil proceedings, often the value of a claim will dictate whether expert evidence can be obtained and tendered to the court (see Chapter 5) thus experts are rarely used in those cases on the small claims track. In contrast, criminal proceedings are governed by the common law and the ultimate issue rule. This states that an expert should not give evidence in relation to an ultimate issue, for example an expert would be prohibited from giving evidence in relation to the mental state of an accused if the ultimate issue is their sanity when they committed the offence. The ultimate issue is a matter for the jury to decide upon, namely did Joan cause Barbara's death. Therefore, the expert is limited in terms of the evidence that he or she can give, this should only relate to those matters that are not directly at issue. The findings of an expert will be given in a report that may be accompanied by oral testimony in court. In civil proceedings these reports are admissible under the CEA 1995 and in criminal proceedings the same is true under s 30 of the CJA 1988.

KEY CASE ANALYSIS: *R v Lowery* [1974] AC 85

Background

A (Lowery) and B (King) were charged with murdering C (Nolte). The issue was who of the two would have actually committed the murder because the evidence pointed to both of them. The prosecution adduced the evidence of a psychiatrist (Professor Cox) in the capacity of an expert who stated that, in his opinion (based on their respective aggression, intelligence and personalities), A was more likely to have committed the murder than B.

Principle established

The evidence was admissible because it related to B's defence that A had killed C.

There are mixed authorities on when expert evidence should and should not be adduced, for instance on matters that the jury may be able to decide upon without help; see *R v Land* [1999] QB 65 concerning expert evidence on the age of a person at the time an offence was committed or *R v Bailey* (1977) 66 Cr App R 31 to evidence **automatism**.

On-the-spot questions

Who qualifies as an expert for the purposes of the law?

Briefly outline the instances in which opinion evidence may be admissible.

Expert evidence as an exception to hearsay

In Chapter 7 the discussion focused on hearsay. The discussion in this chapter highlights that expert opinion evidence is admissible, usually as a written report accompanied by oral testimony. However, in civil proceedings a report produced by a number of experts is admissible as evidence under s 1 of the CEA 1995 and therefore oral testimony is not required. Such a report may be classed as hearsay because the expert who has written it might not have been involved with every part of it or because it is a form of multiple hearsay. In criminal proceedings s 30 of the CJA 1988, ss 114(1)(b) and 127(3) of the CJA 2003 also permit the admission of such reports. You should note that the court may grant leave for the expert not to give evidence; this will only be granted if the court is able to make sense of the report and after it has considered the potential risk of the expert's report not being subject to the scrutiny of the opposition's cross-examination.

Weight

The weight that is attributed to the expert's evidence will depend on the level of competence, experience and skill that they show. The court may refer to the relevant profession for guidance as to what amounts to an expert for its purposes (see *R v Inch* (1989) 91 Cr App R 51).

Neutrality of the evidence

Just because A calls an expert to give evidence on his behalf does not mean that he then has ownership of the evidence that is presented. The expert remains as a witness of the court (see *Harmony Shipping v Saudi Europe Line Ltd* [1979] 1 WLR 1380). The neutrality of this means that both parties may make use of the evidence provided. However, expert evidence may be subject to privilege and therefore the normal rules apply (see Chapter 5). Additionally, in terms of a trial judge's previous acquaintance with an expert see: *Resolution Chemicals Ltd v H Lundbeck A/S* [2013] EWHC 3160.

Disclosure of expert reports

Expert reports are also subject to the rules on disclosure. In civil proceedings Part 35 of the Civil Procedure Rules 2013 governs this issue; all relevant overriding objectives apply, for example efficiency and time saving. In criminal proceedings the Crown Court (Advance Notice of Expert Evidence) Rules 1987 police this area of procedural law; the requirement is to disclose any opinion and method or rationale for it. Failure to comply with these rules may result in the evidence being ruled inadmissible.

Opinion of an accused's general reputation

In civil proceedings and under the common law the doctrine of claim preclusion (res judicata) means that a matter that has already been decided cannot be adjudicated upon once it is concluded. The doctrine bars a party from trying to have the same matter retried. However there are instances in which evidence of previous criminal convictions or findings can be used in subsequent proceedings.

Criminal proceedings

In criminal cases evidence that relates to the character of the accused or others (witnesses or a co-accused) is governed by the CJA 2003 and the PACE Act 1984 (s 74). Sections 98–113 of the CJA 2003 provide for the admissibility of bad character evidence in criminal proceedings. Bad character is defined as '. . . evidence of or towards a disposition towards misconduct' (s 99 of the CJA 2003). The statute abolished some of the common law rules that governed this area of evidence law prior to its enactment, for instance the rules on **similar fact evidence**, however it preserves '. . . any rule of law under which in criminal proceedings evidence of reputation is admissible for the purpose of proving good character, but only so far as it allows the court to treat such evidence as proving the matter concerned' (s 9(2) and s 118(1) of the CJA 2003). In addition, the statute confirmed that evidence or cross-examination in relation to the sexual history of a victim in a case involving a sexual offence continues to be restricted by the YJCEA 1999 and by its own s 112(3)(b). The effect of this provision means that evidence of previous sexual behaviour can only be adduced where the tests outlined in both the YJCEA 1999 and the CJA 2003 are satisfied.

Section 74 of the PACE Act 1984 states that:

> . . . in any proceedings the fact that a person other than the accused has been convicted of an offence by or before any court in the United Kingdom . . . shall be admissible in evidence for the purpose of proving that that person committed that offence, where evidence of his having done so is admissible, whether or not any other evidence of his having committed that offence is given.

The section only applies to criminal convictions following trial rather than those after a plea of guilty (see *R v Golder* [1987] 1 QB 920). This provision is supported by a presumption in favour of the conviction being taken as existing unless the contrary is proven by the opposition (s 74(2)). You should note that the evidence of the previous criminal conviction that is being adduced must be relevant to a matter in issue; where it is not then it is irrelevant and inadmissible. Furthermore, the court's discretion to exclude evidence under s 78 of the PACE Act 1984 applies where the court is of the opinion that the evidence would have an 'adverse effect on the fairness of the proceedings' (see *R v Curry* [1988] Crim LR 527).

Civil proceedings

Civil courts were reticent to accept evidence of a criminal conviction as evidence in civil proceedings; the rationale that underpinned this related to the risk of prejudice that would be created – it was thought that the knowledge of a finding made in a criminal court on a matter may influence the finding that a civil court would make. The logic was flawed because very little is achieved where a civil court is required to go through the same process in relation to a particular point, especially because the standard of proof is lower than that of the criminal courts. To avoid a risk of the court's decision being influenced a criminal conviction can only be used as evidence in specified matters as outlined in s 7 of the CEA 1995 and ss 11–13 of the CEA 1968. These provisions allow evidence relating to the defendant's reputation, previous criminal convictions and findings made in relation to adultery (discussed below) to be adduced in a civil trial. Note that no similar provisions exist in relation to findings in civil cases for the purposes of use in criminal proceedings.

Criminal convictions

Section 11(1) of the CEA 1968 provides:

> . . . in any civil proceedings the fact that a person has been convicted of an offence by or before any court in the United Kingdom . . . shall be admissible in

evidence for the purpose of proving, where to do so is relevant to any issue in those proceedings, that he committed that offence, whether he was so convicted upon a plea of guilty or otherwise and whether or not he is a party to the civil proceedings; but no conviction other than a subsisting one shall be admissible in evidence by virtue of this section.

This provision requires that the criminal conviction must be one by a court of the United Kingdom and that there must be no appeal of the criminal conviction pending. Where a party challenges the criminal conviction then they must prove that it is not relevant or non-existent (see *Taylor v Taylor* [1970] 1 WLR 1148).

Section 11(2) supports s 11(1) and provides that:

> . . . in any civil proceedings in which by virtue of this section a person is proved to have been convicted of an offence . . . he shall be taken to have committed that offence unless the contrary is proved; and . . . for the purpose of identifying the facts on which the conviction was based, the contents of any document which is admissible as evidence of the conviction . . . the contents of the information, complaint, indictment or charge-sheet . . . shall be admissible in evidence for that purpose.

This means that the court presumes the person to have committed the offence unless that person proves the contrary.

Under these provisions the party seeking to rely on the previous criminal conviction must state that they will do so from the outset.

Matrimonial proceedings: a finding of adultery or paternity

Section 12(1) of the CEA 1968 states that:

> . . . in any civil proceedings . . . the fact that a person has been found guilty of adultery in any matrimonial proceedings . . . and the fact that a person has been found to be the father of a child in relevant proceedings before any court in England and Wales shall be admissible in evidence for the purpose of proving, where to do so is relevant to any issue in those civil proceedings, that he committed the adultery to which the finding relates or . . . [he] is (or was) the father of that child, whether or not he offered any defence to the allegation of adultery or paternity and whether or not he is a party to the civil proceedings; but no finding or adjudication other than a subsisting one shall be admissible in evidence by virtue of this section.

Again this requires the finding to have been made by a court in England and Wales.

Section 12(2) provides that:

> . . . in any civil proceedings . . . in which . . . a person is proved to have been
> found guilty of adultery as mentioned or . . . to have been found or adjudged to
> be the father of a child as mentioned . . . he shall be taken to have committed
> the adultery to which the finding relates or, as the case may be, to be (or have
> been) the father of that child, unless the contrary is proved . . . and without
> prejudice to the reception of any other admissible evidence for the purpose of
> identifying the facts on which the finding or adjudication was based, the
> contents of any document which was before the court, or which contains any
> pronouncement of the court, in the other proceedings . . . in question shall be
> admissible in evidence for that purpose.

This means that the court presumes the person to have been adulterous or accepts that a
finding of paternity is made out unless that person proves the contrary.

Again, under these provisions, the party that seeks to rely on the findings must state that
they will do so from the outset.

Conclusiveness of convictions for cases of defamation

Section 13(1) of the CEA 1968 states that:

> . . . in an action for libel or slander in which the question whether the plaintiff
> did or did not commit a criminal offence is relevant to an issue arising in the
> action, proof that, at the time when that issue falls to be determined . . . he
> stands convicted of that offence shall be conclusive evidence that he committed
> that offence; and his conviction thereof shall be admissible in evidence
> accordingly.

Section 13(2) provides that:

> . . . in any such action as aforesaid in which by virtue of this section the plaintiff
> is proved to have been convicted of an offence, the contents of any document
> which is admissible as evidence of the conviction, and the contents of the
> information, complaint, indictment or charge-sheet on which . . . he was
> convicted, shall, without prejudice to the reception of any other admissible
> evidence for the purpose of identifying the facts on which the conviction was
> based, be admissible in evidence for the purpose of identifying those facts.

These final two provisions allow a criminal conviction for libel or slander to be conclusive
evidence that the person convicted committed the offence. Where the presumption applies
in relation to a witness it can be rebutted (see s 12 of the Defamation Act 1996).

On-the-spot questions

In what circumstances will a previous criminal conviction be admissible in a civil claim?

Which statutes regulate the admission of character evidence in criminal proceedings?

Eyewitness opinion

The opinion of eyewitnesses is admissible as evidence. In civil proceedings the evidence of a non-expert witness that conveys an opinion of the facts, as they perceived them to be, is admissible, for instance Joan identifies Jimmy as the person who committed the offence.

SUMMARY

Documentary evidence comes in a variety of forms including emails and faxes. It is considered to be the best form of evidence but there are instances in which the court will accept its inferior cousin, secondary evidence, namely a certified copy for court purposes. Real evidence is tangible and can be visually assessed by the court, for example a kitchen knife or a chapatti pan with which someone was killed as in *DPP v Camplin* [1978] AC 705. Generally, opinion evidence is prohibited save in limited circumstances, including that of an expert witness.

FURTHER READING

Landa, CS (2012). *Evidence: Question and Answers 2013–2014*, 10th edn. London: Routledge.
This textbook focuses on the application of the law of evidence with some interesting practical questions and guidance on answering assessment questions.

Munday, R (2011). *Evidence, Core Text Series*. Oxford: Oxford University Press.
This textbook provides an interesting look at the opinions of psychiatrists in the law courts.

Roberts, A, 'Expert evidence on the reliability of eyewitness identification – some observations on the justifications for exclusion: *Gage v HM Advocate*.' *International Journal of Evidence and Proof*, 2012, 16(1), 93–105.
This article focuses on the possible admission of expert evidence on the reliability of eyewitness evidence in England and Wales after the Scottish case of *Gage v HM Advocate* [2011] HCAJC 40 (HCJ Appeal).

Index

Printed in Great Britain
by Amazon

75382706R00113